THE STORY OF
ARCHITECTURE
THROUGHOUT THE AGES

PLATE I — *The Old Cloth Hall, Ypres*

THE STORY

OF

ARCHITECTURE

THROUGHOUT THE AGES

BY

P. LESLIE WATERHOUSE

YESTERDAY'S CLASSICS

ITHACA, NEW YORK

ISBN: 978-1-63334-167-8

Yesterday's Classics, LLC
PO Box 339
Ithaca, NY 14851

PREFATORY NOTE

AN earlier edition of this book appeared many years ago and claimed a large circle of readers; it has, however, long been out of print. It has now been very fully revised, and in part re-written, and entirely re-illustrated from drawings and prints and from photographs. If in its new form it can open the door of desire, and lead to an increasing interest in buildings new and old, and to a proper appreciation of them, it will serve its purpose.

I am indebted to the Council and Librarian of the Royal Institute of British Architects for the loan of a number of books for illustration. Miss Spiers has kindly lent two water colours (PLATES II and III) from drawings by the late Mr. R. Phené Spiers. I have to thank Mr. Arthur Keen for his drawing of Stokesay Castle (FIGURE 73), and Mr. Marshall Jones, of Boston, has furnished the view of the Woolworth Building, (PLATE XXX). The view shown in PLATE XXXI is from a photograph by Messrs. Aerofilms, Ltd. I have to thank Mr. Fred. Saunders for FIGURE 59, Mr. C. B. Hutchinson for FIGURE 79, and Mr. Louis Ambler for FIGURE 84. The Council of the Architectural Association have also given permission for these to be reproduced from the A.A. Sketch book.

P. L. W.

SHOTOVER, EPSOM.

October, 1924.

CONTENTS

I. EGYPTIAN ARCHITECTURE 1

II. CRETAN AND GREEK ARCHITECTURE . . . 28

III. ETRUSCAN AND ROMAN
ARCHITECTURE 58

IV. EARLY CHRISTIAN ARCHITECTURE 89

V. SARACENIC ARCHITECTURE 110

VI. ROMANESQUE ARCHITECTURE 121

    1. ITALY 121

    2. FRANCE 131

    3. GERMANY 137

    4. SPAIN 140

    5. GREAT BRITAIN 140

VII. GOTHIC ARCHITECTURE 148

    1. FRANCE 156

    2. GREAT BRITAIN 164

    3. ITALY 188

    4. GERMANY 197

    5. BELGIUM, SPAIN, ETC. 199

VIII. RENAISSANCE ARCHITECTURE 201

    1. ITALY 201

    2. FRANCE 223

    3. GREAT BRITAIN 229

IX. MODERN ARCHITECTURE 249

X. ARCHITECTURE TO-DAY 254

    1. AMERICA 259

    2. GREAT BRITAIN 264

BOOKS RECOMMENDED 267

INDEX 275

INTRODUCTION

THERE is no subject that opens to us wide avenues of pleasure at such trifling cost of time as the study of Architecture. And in this field it can be said with truth that a little learning is not a dangerous thing: it is a pleasant and a helpful thing. One may go further and say that for all who wish to get their full share of interest and enjoyment out of life it has become a necessary thing.

Our opportunities for intelligent travel are increasing daily. Less than thirty years ago the motorcar in England was restricted to a pace of four miles an hour; moreover, the law required that it should be preceded by a man waving a red flag. Conditions in this and in other respects have changed in the course of the present century, and our radius of easy travel has enlarged greatly. All thoughtful people are now desiring to acquire an elementary knowledge of the history of the buildings which they may visit in the course of their wanderings, and of the conditions under which these buildings have arisen. And it matters little whether these wanderings be through the towns and villages around their home, or among the greater churches and cathedrals of England, or, further afield, along the banks of the Loire, the Arno, or the Tiber. For it is at last being recognised that Architecture is not a matter of styles and mouldings and students' terms: it has a human quality: it touches us at every point, and, of all the fine arts, is the one most intimately associated with the lives of all of us.

The reader is asked to bear in mind this close association between Architecture and its creators, between Architecture and the civilisation which produced it: to remember that through it, more readily than by any other means, we may grasp the spirit of the past. For Architecture has always been an expression of human life, the medium by which nations have recorded,— truly, because unconsciously,—their emotions, their aspirations, their beliefs. Viewed in this light, old buildings acquire an added charm, as the civilisations which they mark pass in review before us;— Egyptian, Greek or Roman: the genius of the Gothic constructors, expressed in those buildings which represent the "triumph of science and the incarnation of romance"; all the varied energies of the artists of the Renaissance. . . .

And so, down to the present time. For the glamour of the past must not be allowed to blind us to the claims of the present. The Architecture of to-day vitally concerns every householder and every citizen. We must learn,—indeed, we are learning,—to take an intelligent interest in all that is going on around us; to discriminate, to take pride in the glory of every new building in our midst which successfully claims to represent our nobler aspirations. And if, as has been well said, every nation has the Architecture which it deserves, we shall feel that we are, each of us, doing our part and making our contribution towards the "loud sum of the Silent Units."

CHAPTER I

EGYPTIAN ARCHITECTURE

THE earliest men of whom any traces exist were cave-dwellers; and it has been well said that the father of all architecture was he who first discovered that he could build a wall by the simple process of piling one stone upon another. This new idea was followed by the introduction of carpentry, the use of the pier and the lintel, and the many other improvements which went to make true architecture.

A complete story of Architecture would therefore cover almost as great a period of time as the story of man himself. Unfortunately, the efforts of our earlier ancestors in this field have entirely disappeared. It was not until man, in the course of civilisation, became a mighty builder, and not that only, but a builder in materials of an imperishable nature, that he was able to leave behind him monuments to tell the story of his life to future ages. Thus it comes about that it is impossible to trace the growth of the art from its earliest beginnings, and to follow its development as it grew in importance. The oldest memorials of which we have records—the tombs and temples of ancient Egypt—were the work, not of a race of primitive men, but of a nation which had already attained a knowledge of the art of construction which later builders have never surpassed.

The waters of the Nile are the head-waters of architecture. On the banks of this stream—the cradle of the art—the colossal piles of these early builders still command the wonder of all who see them.

Earlier works of the Egyptian builders have been identified, but their greatest and most characteristic monuments, the pyramids of the fourth dynasty, have remained unchallenged for more than five thousand years as the greatest of all architectural undertakings. With these works of the mysterious inhabitants of the Nile valley begins the history of architecture, so far as our knowledge of it can at present go.

No other country bears such testimony as Egypt to the great *historical* value of architecture. Other nations of antiquity have, possibly, been equally powerful, or as highly civilised; but they have failed to leave behind them such enduring monuments to record their greatness—their literature in stone or marble—and they have almost disappeared from the pages of history. Not so the Egyptians. There is a "voicefulness" in these old tombs and temples along the banks of the Nile which gives reality and life to the history of the men who built them. Hence the unique interest which attaches to the architecture of Egypt. These temples, these walls, that have so long been "washed by the passing waves of humanity," present a reliable record of the social and religious life of their builders, whose life-story would otherwise have been totally lost in obscurity. Egypt claims the attention of students of architecture, too, by reason of having produced monuments which, for massiveness and grandeur, have never been excelled in the world's history. Yet Egyptian architecture must ever remain, to some extent, a subject by itself; it occupies no very important place in the story of art, or of the architecture which chiefly concerns us—that of Europe. But as an expression of human character it reflects accurately the intellectual limitations of its designers and constructors. It is a strange fact that, with the exception of the few features which were borrowed by the Greeks, all the characteristic forms of Egyptian architecture have become obsolete; the Greeks, moreover, in adopting any feature, so modified and improved it that it became, in reality, their own. Greece, not Egypt, was the true parent of European architecture; yet the colossal monuments of the Nile valley had weathered thirty centuries before Grecian architecture had left its cradle.

In almost all countries we find that the chief structures are the outcome of the nation's religious beliefs. Such was the case in Egypt from the earliest times. Nothing reveals the character of the nation so clearly as its religion; nothing has a more permeating influence upon its architecture. The Egyptians were a highly civilised, but in no respects an intellectual people; they were essentially religious, with a very lengthy catalogue of deities; they themselves spoke of their "thousand gods," and, in addition to their many principal deities, they paid religious regard to animals.

Cats, dogs and many of the common animals were held sacred; at death their bodies were embalmed, and interred in specially constructed tombs. When a sacred bull, or Apis, died, the funeral would be on an elaborate scale, costing the equivalent of £20,000 of our money. The remains were embalmed, placed in a solid granite sarcophagus weighing fifty tons or more, and deposited in one of the long galleries hewn out of the solid rock.

It will be readily seen, then, that this phase of the nation's religion was productive of a vast amount of architectural work. But of far greater importance in its influence upon the architecture of the country was the belief held by the Egyptians regarding man's life after death. While the bad soul was sentenced to a round of migrations into the bodies of unclean animals, the good soul, as its reward, was made the companion of Osiris for a period of three thousand years. At the end of this time it returned to earth, re-entered its former body, and again lived the life of a human being. Thus it was most desirable that, when the long allotted period had expired, the soul should be able, on returning to earth, to find the body which it was to re-enter.

The natural outcome of this belief was the process of embalming, and the erection of tombs which might be relied upon to last out the span of three thousand years, and to safeguard the body during that period.

The most colossal, and almost the oldest, of these sepulchral monuments are the mysterious structures with which, among the inhabitants of Europe, the name of Egypt has always been associated—the Pyramids.

The largest, and the best known of these are the three at Ghizeh, near Cairo, built respectively by Cheops (or Suphis), Chephren and Mycerinus. The pyramid of Cheops, generally known as the "Great Pyramid," is the most important of the three. Its builder was a tyrant of the fourth dynasty (*circa* 3,500 B.C.), who closed all the temples and forced his subjects to labour for years at this gigantic structure, which was to serve in due course as his tomb. The pyramid has a square base, 755 feet in length, covering an area of about thirteen acres, or twice the extent of St. Peter's at Rome. The four sides were of the form of equilateral triangles, sloping towards and meeting at the top, at a height of 481 feet above the level of the platform. Limestone was chiefly used in its construction, upon a base of solid rock, but over this was an exterior facing of polished granite, every vestige of which has now disappeared. The internal passages are still lined with highly polished granite slabs, fitted together with astonishing accuracy.

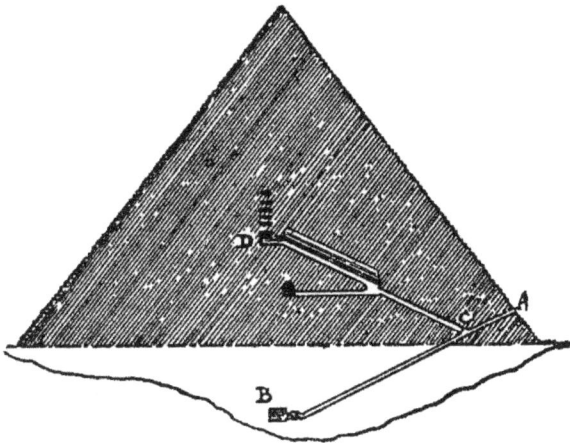

FIGURE I — *Section through the Great Pyramid*

The entrance was at the point marked A, about 47 feet above the original base, and was carefully concealed, extraordinary precautions having been taken to prevent the tomb from being entered. From the entrance a passage slopes down to a chamber, B, cut in the solid rock 120 feet below the natural surface of the ground. The object of this chamber is not apparent; possibly it was intended as a blind. A corridor, turning off at C, leads up to the royal burial-chamber, D, situated almost in the centre of the structure. Below this is a third room, called the "Queen's Chamber," though there is no authority for the name. The chambers and corridors are interesting constructionally, for they show the methods adopted by these early engineers for bridging over openings in order to resist a super-incumbent weight. The central corridor is 28 feet high, with a ceiling formed by courses of masonry which overhang one another successively until they meet at the top. In the case of the "King's Chamber," in which the royal sarcophagus was deposited, marvellous ingenuity was displayed in blocking off the tomb-chamber from the passage, and also in making the roof strong enough to prevent the weight overhead from crushing through. To relieve this weight five enormous slabs were fixed, with a small chamber between each of them; these were surmounted by a rudimentary arch, formed by two massive lintels tilted in such a way as to meet over the centre of the opening.

FIGURE 2 — *Corbelling over King's Chamber*

How this colossal enterprise was carried out in all its details continues to be an excellent subject for speculation. The limestone quarries, which provided the bulk of the stone, were situated at El Massarah, a distance of fifty miles from Ghizeh; the red granite could not have been quarried nearer than Assouan, upon the banks of the Nile, 500 miles away. The blocks of stone could be readily floated down the stream upon rafts; thence it is probable that they were slowly moved into position by means of rollers, being gradually raised to the required height along an inclined plane or embankment constructed for this purpose. It is stated that 100,000 men were employed upon the Great Pyramid for a period of twenty years; so that the raising of such an embankment, though a gigantic undertaking, would represent but a small portion of this vast amount of labour. Many of the blocks of stone measure 30 feet in length and weigh as much as fifty tons, yet they were worked with the greatest exactitude; the polished granite slabs which line the corridors are fitted together with such accuracy that it is almost impossible to detect the joints. Similar accuracy was observed in the setting out of the structure. Professor Petrie's measurements show that the lengths of the sides varied from 755 feet 7.7 inches to 755 feet 9.4 inches, the extreme difference being 1.7 inches only!

Such a vast, unremunerative work could only have been undertaken by a despot with an unlimited amount of labour available. At this period there were few prisoners of war, so that the burden of the task fell mainly upon the shoulders of the King's "free" subjects.

The royal tyrant failed, however, in the one object to which his efforts were directed—the safe preservation of his embalmed remains. The secret of the prison-house was discovered, the tomb rifled, and the royal dust scattered to the four winds of heaven. In the words of Byron's doggerel:

> Let not a monument give you or me hopes,
> Since not a pinch of dust remains of Che-ôps.

The custom of embalming led to the erection of a vast number of smaller tombs, many of which are found in the neighbourhood of the pyramids, for this locality was originally the necropolis of the ancient city of Memphis. These tombs were usually rectangular, with sloping sides, like a pyramid with the top cut off. Internally the walls were decorated with paintings illustrating the everyday life which the occupant had led, the evident intention being to make him feel as much "at home" as possible in his tomb. These paintings have been invaluable in enabling us to realise the exact conditions of life which prevailed at the period. The material employed in the construction of the tombs was limestone, but the constructive methods were evidently borrowed from wooden originals. This imitation, in stone, of wooden methods of construction had a remarkable influence upon later forms of architecture.

It will be seen that the interest attaching to these earliest structures of Egypt is mainly historical, for they can lay claim to little architectural merit, in the true sense of the word. The object which the builders had in view was to make their monuments, not beautiful, but everlasting; and to this end all the refinements were sacrificed. Architecture was treated by them as one of the exact sciences, rather than as a fine art. In the tombs of a later period, however, belonging to the twelfth dynasty (*circa* 2600 B.C.), a more fully developed architectural style is seen. At Beni-Hasan, on the East Bank of the Nile, in Middle Egypt, is a group of tombs of this period, cut in the vertical face of the rock, in which we find the first examples of an important architectural feature, which subsequently influenced the architecture of Greece, and, through it, of Europe.

FIGURE 3 — *Tomb at Beni-Hasan*

The general view of one of these tombs shows a portico with two columns. The whole has been carved out of the solid stone, and two piers have been left in order to give support, or the appearance of support, to the overhanging rock. It will be noticed that the portion above the columns has been squared to the form of a lintel. Over this appears a row of dentils, or tooth-like projections, which are eminently suggestive of the ends of rafters, such as would be used in timber construction. The columns are of a form seldom seen in Egypt; they taper towards the top, and are surmounted

9

by a square slab, or "abacus," which has the appearance of transmitting the weight from the lintel. Some of them are polygonal, with sixteen or thirty-two sides, each side being slightly concave, in the manner of the "flutes" of the Greek columns, which we shall be considering in the next chapter.

If these shafts be compared with the columns of the Greek Doric order (p. 40), it will be seen that there are some notable points of resemblance—the square abacus, the fluted surface, and the tapering outline. A similar form of column was used at a later date at Karnak, but the Egyptians, mighty builders though they were, never grasped the essential principles of fitness and proportion in their architecture, and this column did not find favour with them, and was subsequently discarded by them. Yet this special form was destined to take an important place in the architecture of Europe, for the columns of Beni-Hasan appear to be the prototypes of the columns of the Greek Doric order. It is strange that the discriminating Greeks should have selected, here or elsewhere, for development the very feature which the great Egyptian builders had rejected. Certain it is, however, that the form reappeared, in a less crude state, in the earliest Doric temples of the Greeks about the seventh century B.C., and that, in the hands of the Greek masters, it was afterwards endowed with such beauty and refinement that it became the most perfect architectural feature in existence.

The ceiling of the Beni-Hasan tombs, although cut out of the solid rock, is divided by lintels into three spaces, curved in the form of segments of a circle, in evident imitation of an arched, or vaulted, ceiling. Arched construction finds no place in the great buildings of the Egyptians; but that these old builders were familiar with the true principles of the arch has been proved by the discovery of magnificent brick vaulting of the sixth dynasty (*circa* 3300 B.C.), and the still earlier barrel-vaulted passage in a king's tomb of the third dynasty (*circa* 3900 B.C.), discovered more recently by Professor Flinders Petrie.

FIGURE 4 — *Section through Tomb at Beni-Hasan*

Between the date of the Beni-Hasan tombs and the great Theban period of the eighteenth and nineteenth dynasties—an interval of about eight centuries—little progress appears to have been made in architecture. During part of this period Egypt—or, more correctly, Lower Egypt—was in the hands of the "Shepherd" invaders, of whom we know little. Throughout their long rule they were hated by the Egyptians, and they left few permanent memorials behind them; but with the expulsion of the "Shepherd" kings began an era of great architectural activity lasting for three hundred years, down to the period assigned to the exodus of the Jews (*i.e.* from 1600 to 1300 B.C.). This was the great temple-building age, the "Theban period," which witnessed the culmination of Egyptian power and artistic greatness, and produced the greater number of the noblest buildings in the country. Constructively, however, there was a falling-off from the precision and careful work of the earlier periods. The masonry was hastily and clumsily wrought, angles were inaccurately set out, and columns irregularly spaced; in many respects the work bears marks of carelessness and haste which detract considerably from its merit. In spite of technical defects, however, the buildings of this period were noble works which still remain the chief glory of Egyptian architecture.

The cause of this architectural revival is not far to seek. Before the period of the "Shepherd" kings, and during their rule, the inhabitants of the Nile valley had not been a fighting nation. But when Aahmes ascended the throne of Upper Egypt (*circa* 1600 B.C.), he set himself the task of ridding the country of the invaders, and, after pursuing them into Palestine, completely routed them. As a result of this victory, many thousands of slaves were brought back by the king on his return to Egypt. These advantages, and various successes over the Syrians, whetted the appetites of the Egyptians for further conquests, and they henceforth became a nation of conquerors. Under Thothmes III (*circa* 1450 B.C.), their "sphere of influence" advanced by leaps and bounds. Each year witnessed new expeditions, which brought into the country not only enormous quantities of treasure, but vast numbers of prisoners of war—for the object of the king was to capture rather than to kill. This wholesale importation of captives had an immediate effect upon the architecture of the country. By their forced labour, Thothmes was enabled to erect temples and other vast structures which placed him in the first rank of Egyptian builders.

The great city of this period was Thebes—the "hundred-gated Thebes" of Homer—which was practically the capital of the country. Memphis, situated farther north, nearer to the delta of the Nile, vied with Thebes in the magnificence of its temples; but its remains which have come down to us are comparatively unimportant, owing to the fact that the site has been used as a quarry for the supply of materials to Cairo and adjoining modern towns. Thebes, however, was more fortunately situated; no great city has sprung up in its neighbourhood, and its buildings have suffered only from the wasting hand of time, more merciful than that of man.

The great building monarchs of the Theban period were Thothmes III, Amenhotep III, Seti I and Rameses II, each of whom endeavoured to surpass the efforts of his predecessor with some "new temple, nobler than the last." Their names, it will be seen, appear in connection with the greatest temple structures of this era.

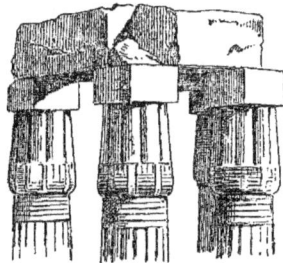

FIGURE 5 — *Lotus-bud Capitals, Luxor*

The most imposing of all the Theban buildings was the great temple at Karnak, 1,200 feet long, around which were grouped several smaller ones; at Luxor, two miles farther south, was another vast palace-temple. The groups on the opposite bank of the river included the sepulchral temple of Amenhotep III—second only to that of Karnak—and the Ramessium, built entirely by the great Rameses.

The principal work of Thothmes was the rebuilding of a portion of the great temple at Karnak. Isolated examples of this master-builder's work are familiar to Europeans. In front of the grand entrance to the temple at Karnak he erected two obelisks; one of these, which now stands before the church of S. John Lateran in Rome, is the largest and most splendid monument of its kind extant. He built, or added to, temples at Heliopolis, Abydos, Denderah, Memphis and many other places, both in Egypt and in Nubia. An obelisk of this monarch has been re-erected at Constantinople; another, which stood originally at Heliopolis and afterwards at Alexandria, is now to be seen on the Thames Embankment, where we know it as "Cleopatra's Needle"; its companion has crossed the Atlantic and has been erected in New York.

Amenhotep continued the building of the temple at Karnak, and erected a vast new temple, of which, however, hardly a trace remains, for it has suffered from the inundations of the Nile; but an enduring memorial of the king, and of an architect bearing the same name, survives in the two mutilated colossi, fifty-six feet high,

PLATE II — *Hall of Columns, Karnac*

PLATE III — *Temple of Ramses, Karnac*

of which one has been known, since the days of the Greeks, as the "vocal Memnon."

By far the greatest and most impressive of all the buildings of this period was the grand temple of Ammon at Karnak. Like many of our mediæval cathedrals, this was the work of successive kings and generations; its walls and columns, covered with inscriptions, furnish almost a complete history of the Theban kings.

The temple was begun by Usertesen I, the great king of the twelfth dynasty (*circa* 2400 B.C.). After an interval of several centuries, Thothmes I continued the work, adding a courtyard surrounded by a colonnade of Osirid pillars. Thothmes III constructed a magnificent columnar hall, 143 feet by 53 feet—dimensions which had never before been approached in a building of this form. He also set to work to restore the ancient sanctuary of Usertesen, reverently preserving all the lines of the old building, and recording the details of the restoration in an inscription on the walls. But the great glory of the temple was the Hypostyle Hall, begun by Rameses I (*circa* 1350 B.C.), but built chiefly by Seti I. This was the most imposing structure in the world's history, and is familiar to all travellers in modern Egypt. The hall measured 340 by 170 feet, its massive roof being carried by 134 columns in sixteen rows; the shafts of the two central rows, which supported the higher portion of the roof, were more than 60 feet high and almost 12 feet in diameter. "No language," writes Fergusson, "can convey an idea of its beauty, and no artist has yet been able to reproduce its form so as to convey to those who have not seen it an idea of its grandeur. The mass of its central piers, illumined by a flood of light from the clerestory, and the smaller pillars of the wings gradually fading into obscurity, are so arranged and lighted as to convey an idea of infinite space; at the same time the beauty and massiveness of the forms, and the brilliancy of their coloured decorations, all combine to stamp this as the greatest of man's architectural works, but such a one as it would be impossible to reproduce, except in such a climate and in that individual style in which, and for which, it was created."

This wonderful hall was almost entirely built during the reign of Seti I. Upon his death, it was completed by his son, Rameses II, better known to Bible-readers as the Pharaoh of the Oppression. He added the fifty-four columns on the south side. In the methods of construction there are distinct evidences of deterioration as compared with much of the work of the more ancient Egyptians. Where, at an earlier date, monolithic columns of red granite would have been used, we find at this period soft sandstone built up in drums. Thus, in order to insure the strength of the columns, it was necessary to make them excessively massive, and by this they lost more of grace than they gained in dignity.

It would have been impossible for the Egyptian monarchs to erect such stupendous structures but for the fact that they were able, through their victorious wars, to bring into the country vast numbers of captives, whose lives were spent in forced labour upon these public works. In a series of interesting tomb-drawings, referring to the building of this temple at Karnak, we find depicted the tasks upon which the prisoners were continually occupied. Some are busy kneading clay; others either make bricks in wooden moulds, or spread them in rows to bake; others carry on the building operations. By the side are explanations of the drawings; part of the inscription is worth quoting: "We see the captives who were carried away as prisoners in very great numbers; they work at the building with skilful fingers. Their overseers show themselves in sight: these attend with strictness, obeying the word of the great skilful lord of the works; . . . they are rewarded with wine and all kinds of good dishes; they perform their service with a mind full of love for the king; they build for Thothmes III a holy of holies. May it be rewarded to him through a number of many endless years! The overseer speaks thus to the labourers at the building:

'The stick is in my hand; be not idle.'" Such a picture enables us to realise the conditions under which these colossal buildings laboriously came into existence—the slave population toiling unceasingly at the point of the goad, while the task-masters, by their exacting severity, earned for themselves a share of the good things of this life.

After the period of the Exodus (*circa* 1300 B.C.), a change came over the land; the Egyptians lost a great number of their slaves, and, as a result or a coincidence, the era of temple-building practically ended with the reign of the great Rameses.

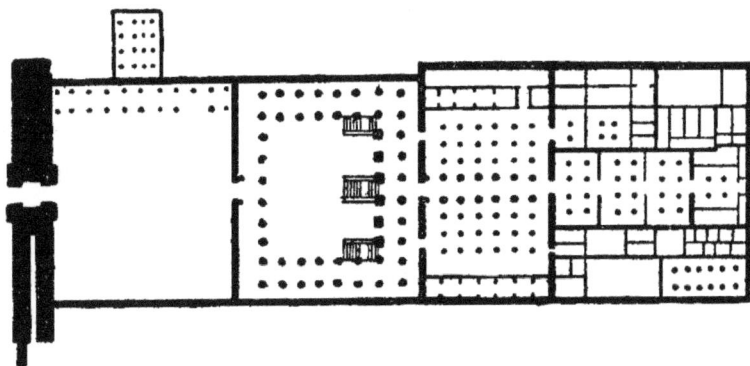

FIGURE 6 — *Plan of Ramessium*

At Karnak the chief object of each monarch was to surpass, in extent and magnificence, the buildings of his predecessors, without regard to congruity of plan. But in the Ramessium at Thebes, a temple wholly built by the great Rameses, we see the plan of a typical temple of the period. The façade was formed by two massive pyramidal towers (pylons), between which was the entrance doorway; in many cases this façade was situated obliquely with regard to the temple building. The doorway gave access to a great fore-court, flanked by colonnades, which in turn led to an inner court, smaller than the first, but more richly decorated with statuary. Both courts were open to the sky.

Beyond these we reach the Hypostyle Hall—the chief feature in the larger temples. In the centre of this, two rows of lofty columns supported the higher portion of the roof, the remainder of the space being occupied by ranges of smaller columns. The central portion of the roof was higher than that at the sides, an arrangement which allowed light to be admitted through perforated stone panels, fixed in the wall, which connected the upper portion of the roof with the lower, in the manner of the clerestory windows of Gothic architecture. Beyond this hall were several smaller chambers, which appear to have been set apart for use by the king or the priests.

The columns were brilliantly coloured, and their capitals were varied to suit the positions in which they were placed, with due regard to the light; those of the lofty and well-lighted central pillars were bell-shaped, but the columns at the side had bud-shaped capitals— wide at the base and tapering towards the top—a form which allowed the decoration, lighted from above, to be seen to advantage.

After the Exodus ensued a long period of decay and inactivity lasting for almost a thousand years, until the old glories of Egypt were, to some extent, revived by the Ptolemies. Under their rule and, later, under the Romans, the land enjoyed again a season of great prosperity. Temples were erected which vied in size and splendour with those of the great Theban age. Of these, none is more beautiful than the temple of Isis at Philæ, the plan of which is a striking illustration of the disregard of accuracy and of regularity which characterised many buildings of the Egyptians, The Greeks and the Romans were accustomed to set out their works with great accuracy; but at Philæ the Egyptians evidently worked to their own methods, for there are hardly two parallel walls, or a right angle, in the building. Imposing temples of this period are found also at Denderah and at Edfou—the latter the most perfectly preserved temple in Egypt. As evidence of the conservatism of this old nation of builders, it is interesting to note that the structures of this period bear no trace of Greek or Roman influence, either in the architectural details or in the decorations which covered the walls; so that, until their true place in history was assigned to them through the interpretation of the hieroglyphic inscriptions, some of the Ptolemaic buildings were considered to be anterior to those of the great Theban period.

Egyptian civilisation was, in fact, a matter of routine. During thousands of years there was no great intellectual awakening in the art and architecture of these mighty builders; there was little development or growth. "The civilisation that we find before us in the earliest known history," writes Professor Petrie, "appears elaborate and perfect. Few discoveries of importance were made during the thousands of years which ensued."

But the buildings which remain to us are wonderfully impressive, and shed a vivid light upon the habits and lives, as well as upon the limitations, of these early Egyptians.

We have seen that in the temple-structures of the Egyptians one of the most important features was the column. Its constant use within the buildings was probably encouraged, as tending to add to the prevailing air of mystery which the priests made it their business to foster. To some extent it was necessitated by the constructive system employed, for the great stone slabs which formed the roof required strong support at frequent intervals. The column thus gradually became the chief medium for obtaining decorative effect.

Many varieties were used; they were invariably massive, and rarely exceeded six diameters in height. The shaft tapered towards the top, and was usually either circular or clustered; sometimes it was fluted, as at Beni-Hasan. In many examples the column was reduced in diameter at the base, the point where the greatest strength was required; this, and the use, above the capital, of an abacus of smaller dimensions than the shaft itself, tended to give it an overgrown, bulky appearance, making it look, as it were, weak through excess of strength. The chief forms of capitals in use were: (*a*) the bell-shaped capital (central columns, Karnak), which produced many graceful forms, and to which, as we shall see later, the early Corinthian capitals of the Greeks bore a striking resemblance; (*b*) the clustered lotus bud, representing a cluster of unopened buds of the lotus flower (with this capital a clustered

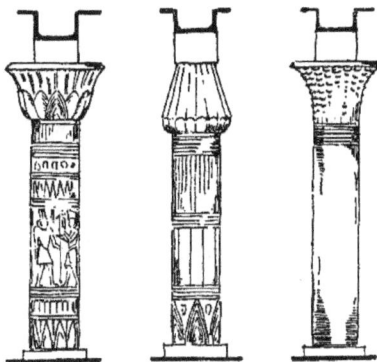

FIGURE 7 — *Egyptian Columns*

column was used); and (c) the palm capital. Most of these forms, were derived from plant life. In Egypt, at the present day, bundles of reed plastered with mud may frequently be seen in use as columns; several small bundles, each tightly bound, are banded together and form a shaft sufficiently rigid to support heavy weights. This primitive arrangement was copied, probably first in wood, and later in stone, and is undoubtedly the origin of the clustered and banded lotus column.

For the interior of the temples colour, rather than form, was relied upon for decorative effect. In the dim light of the columnar halls, mouldings and carving could not have been seen to advantage, and brilliant colouring was essential. The walls and columns were covered with a profusion of hieroglyphic inscriptions and of paintings, in which the designs were either outlined or cut in low relief before the colour was applied. Where coarse sandstone had been used in the erection of the building, a smooth surface for the colour was obtained by the use of stucco, with which the imperfections of the stone were filled up.

Akin in antiquity to the civilisation of the Nile valley was that of the great Kingdom of Assyria, comprising the fertile plains of the Tigris and Euphrates, and the joyous Mesopotamia, which has become a familiar name in recent times. Here was Ur of the Chaldees, the old city of Abraham, where recent excavations have been yielding interesting results and have disclosed remains of mighty buildings of *circa* 2400 B.C. Of even greater antiquity are the remains of the temple at Tell El Obeid, near Ur, with its columns overlaid with copper and its mosaics. The discoveries on this site suggest a Babylonian civilisation as early as 5000 B.C., and show us possibly the oldest examples of buildings at present known.

Unlike the monumental structures of Egypt, the Assyrian remains have survived only in a fragmentary state, for little save the foundations is left of the enormous palaces of this once mighty kingdom. Excavations which have been carried on at Nineveh the capital, and at Khorsabad, have revealed almost complete plans of the royal dwellings, showing that they were of remarkable extent and magnificence. Portions of the great gateway of the palace of Khorsabad may be seen in the British Museum. The immense scale of this portal, with its human-headed winged bulls 19 feet high, enables us to form some opinion of the massive grandeur which characterised these vast buildings of the Assyrians. Owing to the extensive use of sun-dried bricks in lieu of harder materials, the structures lacked the durability of the Nile valley temples. So far as can be determined from the bas-reliefs and the structural remains, the architecture—apart from the applied ornamental forms—had comparatively little artistic merit.

That the Assyrians, like the Egyptians, understood the principles of the arch has been proved by a fine arched gateway, discovered by M. Place at Khorsabad, and by remains of arched drains and of brick vaulting. On existing bas-reliefs are found representations of domed buildings, from which it may be assumed that this form of roof was not unknown, though it is improbable that it was used to any extent.

The prominent feature in Egyptian temples—the column—did not occupy an important place in the architecture of the Assyrians; with the exception of the bas-reliefs, the existing remains reveal no trace of its use. On the sculptures a form of column, with small volutes, is represented, which may claim to be the prototype of the column of the Greek Ionic order. The interior walls of the palaces were lined, to the height of about 10 feet, with alabaster slabs, on which were represented, in low relief, battle and hunting scenes and mythological subjects. Many of these slabs are to be found in the chief museums of Europe.

FIGURE 8 —
Assyrian Column

With the Persians who, under Cyrus (536 B.C.), became masters of these older monarchies, another style of architecture was developed, which attained great magnificence under Darius and Xerxes. Before their period of conquest the Persians had been simple in their mode of life, with little architecture of their own. Under later monarchs, very different in character from the great conqueror Cyrus, they acquired luxurious habits, and soon surpassed even the Assyrians in the splendour and the extent of their palaces. Persian splendour and luxury culminated in the great capital at Persepolis, or Takht-i-Jamshyd (the Throne of Jamshyd), as it is still called by the inhabitants of the district, after its mythical founder and ruler. In the treasury of this great city it is said that Alexander, on his entry, found wealth to the amount of thirty millions sterling.

Here the chief buildings rested upon vast platforms and terraces carved out of the solid rock, which still remain, while almost every vestige of the mighty halls and palaces which covered them has disappeared. With the exception of a few ruins, hardly a monument remains to mark the desolate site of the old luxurious civilisation:

> The Lion and the Lizard keep
> The Courts where Jamshyd gloried and drank deep:
> And Bahràm, that great Hunter—the Wild Ass
> Stamps o'er his head, but cannot break his sleep.

The great Hall of Xerxes at Persepolis was undoubtedly one of the most extensive and imposing buildings of ancient times, having an area of 350 by 300 feet, or almost twice the area of the great Hypostyle Hall at Karnak. Its roof was supported by lofty columns, no less than 64 feet in height, 4 feet 6 inches in diameter, fluted and slightly tapering. Many of the capitals were of remarkable design, in the shape of a double bracket, formed by the forepart of two bulls placed back to back. Frequently between the bracket and the column, as in the illustration, a bell-shaped capital was introduced— very similar to one of the Egyptian forms—and, above this, a weak and clumsy feature consisting of a bundle of vertical scrolls. These scrolls are not unlike the volutes of the Greek Ionic Capital (p. 50), but set vertically instead of horizontally. The wooden beams which supported the roof appear to have rested in the hollow space between the necks of the bulls. These curious capitals may be seen in the rock-cut tomb of Darius, carved out of the foot of the mountain adjoining the terraces, in which is represented, on a small scale, a copy of one of these colossal halls.

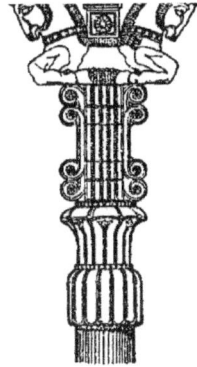

FIGURE 9 — *Capital from Persepolis*

But although the vast empire of Persia, stretching from the Indus on the east to Thrace and Egypt on the west, absorbed almost every kingdom with which its hosts came into conflict, its architecture had little influence upon succeeding styles, or upon that of Europe. Far different might have been the result had the invading hordes overflowed Europe, and not been successfully resisted by those brave Greeks who

Breasted, beat Barbarians, stemmed Persia rolling on,
Did the deed, and saved the world, for the day was Marathon!

CHAPTER II

CRETAN AND GREEK ARCHITECTURE

UNTIL recent years it was generally accepted as a fact that while Egypt, by its imposing architectural monuments, revealed to us a civilisation dating back thousands of years before our era, Europe was, by contrast, the real "Dark Continent," which had not at that time emerged from its primitive conditions. The discoveries in Crete have, however, opened out a new horizon and have given us a new standpoint from which to survey early European history. In the remains of the mighty palaces of Knossos and elsewhere in Crete it has been possible to trace a European civilisation co-equal with that of Egypt, and in some respects surpassing in its achievements the works of the early Egyptian builders.

Sir Arthur Evans, who has been so successful in his Cretan excavations, has made this subject peculiarly his own, so that we may be allowed to use his own words to illustrate the importance of the discoveries made by himself and his fellow-explorers. To this early civilisation he applied the name of "Minoan," from Minos, the legendary king and law-giver of Crete, and this term has been generally accepted.

"The marvellous Minoan civilisation," he writes, "that has there come to light shows that Crete of four thousand years ago must unquestionably be regarded as the birthplace of our European civilisation in its higher form..... Moreover, most recent investigations have more and more brought home the all pervading community between Minoan Crete and the land of the Pharaohs. When we realise the great indebtedness of the succeeding classical culture of Greece to its Minoan predecessor, the full significance of this conclusion will be understood. Ancient Egypt can no longer be regarded as something apart from general human history."

This high early culture, the equal rival of Egypt and Babylonia, which thus began to take its rise in Crete in the fourth millennium before our era, flourished for some two thousand years, eventually dominating the Aegean and a large part of the Mediterranean basin.

It is difficult in a few words to do adequate justice to this earliest of European civilisations. Its achievements are too manifold. The many-storied palaces of the Minoan priest-kings in their great days, by their ingenious planning, their successful combination of the useful with the beautiful and stately, and last but not least, by their scientific sanitary arrangements, far outdid the similar works, on however vast a scale, of Egyptian or Babylonian builders.

"The modernness of much of the life here revealed is astonishing. The elaboration of the domestic arrangements, the staircases storey above storey, the front places given to ladies at the shows, their fashionable flounced robes and jackets, the gloves sometimes seen on their hands or hanging from their folding chairs, their very mannerisms as seen on the frescoes . . . how strangely out of place would it all appear in a classical design.

Nowhere, not even at Pompeii, have more living pictures of ancient life been called up for us than in the Minoan palace of Knossos." [1]

The chief sites excavated in Crete are Knossos, Phæstos and Gournia. Of these Knossos is the most famous and the most accessible; its palace was a "town in itself," standing four storeys high, with two great courts, a theatre area, audience chambers, bath rooms, and a "drainage system not equalled in Europe between that day and the nineteenth century." [2]

This world-famous piece of territory, including the site of the Great Palace, has been throughout this century the property of Sir Arthur Evans, who, in the generous spirit in which he has carried out the whole of his archæological work, has recently made over his rights, as owner and excavator, to the British School at Athens.

The palace was twice destroyed and was remodelled on a greater scale than ever in the "golden age of Crete" (*circa* 1500 B.C.), but within half a century it fell to the destroyer, and with it the era of splendour at Knossos came to an end. Meanwhile Mycenæ and Tiryns were becoming important centres on the mainland, and with

[1] Evans, "New Archæological Lights, etc."

[2] Hawes, "Crete: the Forerunner of Greece."

PLATE IV — *Staircase to the Upper Storeys,*
Great Palace at Knossos

the steady decline in prosperity and in art which ensued at Crete the supremacy was gradually transferred to these capitals.

The earliest traces of civilisation and architecture on the mainland of Europe date back little further than the age of Homer and of Troy; of Atreus, Agamemnon and the other heroes of the Trojan war (*circa* 1180 B.C.). This architecture was an offshoot from Minoan Crete. The most important of the remains are found at Tiryns, the mythical city of Perseus, and at Mycenæ, the capital, according to Homer, of Atreus and Agamemnon. Of the men who lived there before these times, and of their civilisation, we know nothing; they have all, as Horace tells us, passed into oblivion:

Brave men have lived in times of old,
   'Ere Agamemnon first drew breath;
But ah! no bard their praises told,
   And all are lost in nameless death.

They lacked, however, not only the sacred bard, but also that more trustworthy historian of antiquity—the architect. The brave men who lived before Aga-memnon left no enduring architecture behind them, and their history—unlike that of the old Egyptians—is a sealed book to us. A few monuments of Aga-memnon's period still exist, and supply the only reliable information which we possess of the history of that time; but our knowledge of them must ever remain scanty.

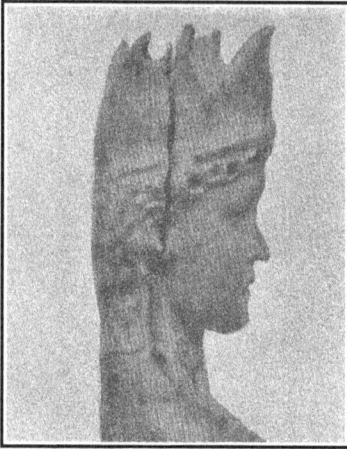

PLATE V — *Head of Ivory Statuette, Mid-Minoan Period circa 1700–1550* B.C.

Homer, indeed, sang bravely of the deeds of these men, but in the writings of the old poets it is impossible to separate facts from fiction. "The age of Homer," as Ruskin tells us, "is surrounded with darkness, his very personality with doubt. Not so that of Pericles; and the day is coming when we shall confess that we have learnt more of Greece out of the crumbled fragments of her sculpture than even from her sweet singers or soldier historians."

The Golden Age of Crete, it has been well said, was

the precursor of the Golden Age of Greece, but we have little authentic Grecian history before the date of the first Olympiad (776 B.C.). The few remains of an earlier date than this are therefore of great interest. These early structures consist chiefly of fortifications, tombs and walls.

PLATE V — *Griffin Fresco in so-called Throne Room, Knossos Late Minoan Period circa 1500 B.C.*

Remains of walls are found in many parts of the country—Cyclopean masonry, as it is called, for the method of construction was suggestive of the work of giants, and tradition ascribed its origin to the Cyclopes. The chief feature of the work is the employment of enormous blocks of stone, sometimes irregularly shaped, but usually coursed and fitted together without mortar. At Tiryns the acropolis is surrounded by a wall of this character; a similar wall at Mycenæ contains the great Gate of Lions, probably the most ancient example extant of Greek sculpture. This gateway consists of two monolithic piers and a massive lintel; the wall was

33

"corbelled" over in such a way that the lintel was relieved from its weight, the triangular space thus formed being filled in with a sculptured group representing two lions supporting a column which tapers from the top towards the base.

FIGURE 10 — *Lion Gate, Mycenæ*

The earliest existing structure in Greece, possessing architectural merit, and of regular form, is the so-called Treasury of Atreus at Mycenæ. This is in reality a tomb, consisting of two subterranean chambers in communication with one another. The larger chamber is shaped like a beehive, roofed over with a kind of dome, composed of massive blocks of stone laid without mortar. The builders appear to have been unacquainted with the use of the arch, for

FIGURE 11 — *Section through the Treasury of Atreus*

although the roof is domical in form, as seen from the interior, the structural method adopted differs from arched, or true domical construction in a most material point. The stones—as in the Lion Gate and other openings in the old walls of the acropolis—are not built in the radiating form of a true arch, but are laid in a series of horizontal courses, so that each course overhangs the one below it; the space is thus gradually narrowed until the projecting courses meet at the top— an arrangement similar to the roofs over the galleries in the Pyramids. Immense blocks of stone are used in the structure; the lintel over the inner doorway is a single block 27 feet long and 16 feet deep, weighing not less than 120 tons. The chief architectural feature of the building was the entrance doorway flanked by shafts entirely covered with elaborate zig-zag ornamentation, showing a fairly developed style. The largest portions of these shafts, after having been lost, were re-discovered and are now set up in a restored form in the British Museum.

These earlier works in Greece differ entirely in form and construction from the later development of true Greek architecture. Hellenic civilisation resulted from a mingling of various races who migrated into Greece. Achæans came first, then Æolians and Dorians, the last of whom over-ran Crete also, and overwhelmed the Minoan dynasty there about 1000 B.C. The resulting Hellenes were never united as one people, but formed a series of states, which developed a great civilisation; and it was the art which they evolved—the "classical architecture" of Greece, as it is called—which has been the parent of all the styles throughout Europe in succeeding centuries.

The period during which this architecture flourished was a comparatively short one, for the date of the oldest known building—a temple of the Doric order at Corinth—is not earlier than 650 B.C. For two centuries after this, art progressed until, after the defeat of the Persians, it reached its culmination at Athens during the great Periclean age (460–400 B.C.). A period of reaction then ensued, followed by a short-lived but splendid revival under Alexander the Great, and, on his death (323 B.C.), by a decline from which it never recovered.

The buildings throughout these periods upon which the ancient Greeks lavished their genius were the temples. These differed from the temples of the old Egyptians in almost all points save one—the frequent use of the column as the dominant feature of the design. But the Egyptians built their temples with a view to impress the worshipper by the mystery, the richness, and the grandeur of the interior; for this reason, and for constructive purposes, the columns were placed *inside* the building. With the Greeks, on the other hand, the temples were comparatively small; they were not built as vast memorials of the greatness of despotic monarchs, nor were they required for the accommodation of crowds of worshippers. The roofs had not the massive solidity of the Egyptian structures, and few supports were necessary; moreover, the buildings were designed for external effect. In the Greek temples, therefore, the principal columns were ranged on the *outside.*

As a rule, the building occupied a conspicuous position, that it might be visible from all points and be admired by all. The Greeks' form of worship was not congregational; it consisted chiefly in prayers offered up outside the sanctuary—from any point within view of the temple—to the deity whose image was enshrined in it. To provide shelter for this image was, in fact, the chief purpose of the temple. Thus the plan was invariably simple. In the smaller buildings, four walls formed an oblong chamber, the *naos,* in which was placed the statue of the deity. A portico with columns, the *pronaos,* gave access to this

FIGURE 12 — *Plan of Small Greek Temple*

chamber; the whole stood upon a platform, and was covered by a simple roof terminating in a gable at each end. In the larger temples, as we shall see later in the Parthenon, columns were ranged all round, forming a peristyle, and at the back of the sacred cell a second chamber was sometimes added, to serve probably as a treasury in which to deposit the votive offerings. Stone, frequently marble, was the material used in the construction throughout, except in the roofs, which were of wood covered with marble tiles. The perishable roofs have all disappeared, and with them has been lost all evidence regarding the method adopted by the Greeks for the lighting of the temples; for with one exception—the great temple at Agrigentum—the walls of all known buildings of this kind were windowless. The question of the lighting of the Greek temple has given rise to much speculation, the most acceptable

37

theory being that the light was admitted through a row of windows high up over the internal colonnades.

Reference has already been made to the "Doric order" of Greek architecture, and throughout this story we shall constantly have to refer to the "classical orders." The term requires a few words of explanation.

To the casual observer, Greek temples would all bear a striking resemblance to one another; yet among the designs there existed three quite distinct styles. Each style was marked by the use of its peculiar form of column, and, accompanying this, was a series of mouldings and proportions, found only in conjunction with that column. Among the Greeks the "three orders" were called the Doric, the Ionic and the Corinthian. The Doric order, the earliest of the three, was marked by simplicity, strength, severity; the Ionic was more graceful and ornate; and the Corinthian, the last to make its appearance, still more rich and exuberant in detail. The Corinthian order had hardly established itself before Greece came under the sway of Rome; but with the Romans, who adopted and remodelled the architecture of Greece, it became the most popular, as well as the most beautiful, of the orders.

The earliest example of the Doric order in Greece is the temple at Corinth (650 B.C.), the oldest Greek temple of which we have any record. Several columns of this building, carrying a portion of the entablature, still stand, and show the design to be somewhat crude, yet with all the characteristic features of the order; the columns are monolithic, stumpy and massive. Later examples show marked improvement in proportion and workmanship. In the Theseum, or so-called temple of Theseus, at Athens (465 B.C.), for example, the shafts are more slender and the mouldings more refined. But it was not until the time of the Persian wars that the noblest architecture of Greece was developed, when the Athenians gave vent to their enthusiasm, after the invaders had been defeated, by the rebuilding of the national monuments.

Under the wise rule of Pericles (445–431 B.C.), a glorious period of activity ensued, when architecture in Greece culminated, and the unrivalled group of national buildings sprang up on the Acropolis at Athens. Foremost among these was the Doric temple of the virgin goddess Athene, the world-renowned Parthenon (Gr. *parthenos,* a virgin), a building which, for beauty of design and for delicacy of workmanship, must by regarded as the nearest approach to perfection of all works ever erected by man.

The Parthenon reveals to us all the leading features of a fully developed Doric temple. The plan, as we see,

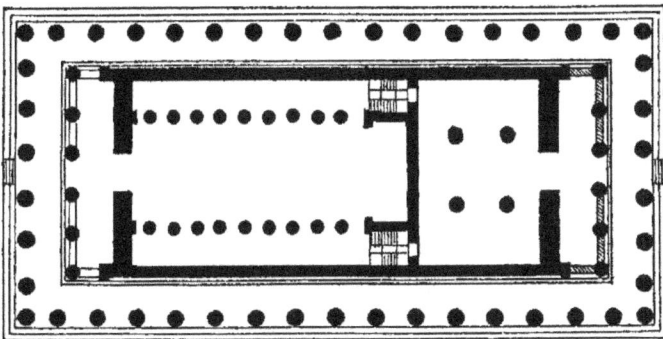

FIGURE 13 — *Plan of the Parthenon*

was simple and regular, consisting of two cells—the sacred chamber and a small treasury behind it. Round these was ranged a peristyle, or series of columns, eight of which formed a portico at each end; each portico contained an inner row of six columns. The whole structure stood upon a "stylobate," or raised pavement, three steps in height.

In conjunction with this plan, let us consider the features which constitute a design of the Doric order. The column of this order, as the illustration shows, has no base, but is set directly upon the stone floor or platform; its diameter is greatest at the foot, and from this point it tapers towards the top not in a straight line, but with a subtle convex curve, or swelling, called the "entasis." Around the shaft are flutes, or shallow channels, twenty, or sometimes sixteen in number, with a sharp edge between them. Surmounting the shaft is a plain, sturdy capital, made up of a square slab, or "abacus," upon which the superstructure rests, with a circular cushion called the "echinus," spreading out from the top of the shaft to receive the weight from the abacus. The grooves on the face of the column are carried up until they are checked by a band of fillets just below the capital.

FIGURE 14 —
The Doric Order

The upper portion of the design, supported by the columns, is called the entablature. This consists, first of a horizontal marble beam, or "architrave," upon

40

which the weight rests, and by which it is distributed to the columns. Being the *supporting* member of the entablature, the architrave was almost invariably left plain, lest ornamentation of its surface should detract from its appearance of strength. Above the architrave runs the frieze, which, in the Doric order, was divided into square panels, or "metopes," separated by slightly projecting blocks, called "triglyphs" (three channels), on the face of which are cut vertical grooves. As will be seen from the sketch, a triglyph occurs over each column, and one between each pair of columns. In many cases the metopes were filled in with sculpture in relief. The remaining portion of the entablature, above the frieze, is the "cornice."

FIGURE 15 — *The Parthenon Restored*

We see, then, that the leading features of the order are the column and its entablature, the latter consisting of three parts—the plain architrave, the frieze, with its metopes and triglyphs, and the cornice. On the

41

underside of the cornice will be noticed a series of marble slabs (mutules), each having a number of small projections resembling wooden pins, or nail heads.

At the ends of the building the upper members of the cornice are made to follow the lines of the sloping roof until they meet in the centre at the top, while the lower portion is carried along horizontally above the frieze. The triangular space thus formed is called the pediment; and, as the most prominent part of the design, contained the finest of the sculpture with which the temples were frequently adorned.

The main details of the Doric order appear to have been derived from early forms of construction in timber. The architrave represents the beam which would be found in a similar position in a wooden building; the triglyphs correspond to the ends of cross-beams, made up of three planks, or perhaps grooved for decorative

PLATE VIII — *Doric Temple of Concord at Girgenti (Agrigentum)*

effect; and there seems little reason to doubt that the mutules are reminiscences of the sloping ends of rafters studded with nails. The other feature, however—the column—does not suggest a wooden prototype; as we have before noticed, it is possible that the tombs of Beni-Hasan, or the temples of the Nile valley—or more probably the temple buildings of Crete—furnished the rough models from which the Greeks evolved this, the most dignified feature of their architecture.

We have mentioned the Parthenon as the noblest

PLATE VII — *North-East Angle of the Parthenon*

example of a temple of the Doric order. Careful measurements of this building have revealed the existence of a number of refinements in its construction—with a view to the correction of optical illusions—which help us to appreciate the extraordinary thought and care which the Greeks bestowed on their designs. The best known of these refinements is the "entasis," or swelling of the outlines of the columns. The bounding lines of the shaft, which appear straight, are in reality convex—curved outwards from the straight line—to the extent only of three-quarters of an inch in a height of more than 31 feet. This curve is not noticeable to the eye, but is just sufficient to counteract the tendency which exists in a straight-sided column to look hollow in the middle.

Again, the underside of the architrave appears to be perfectly straight. Now a long, horizontal line, which is perfectly straight, tends to look as though it "sags" or droops in the centre. To compensate for this, the horizontal lines of the entablature are all slightly curved upwards towards the centre, deviating from a straight line to the extent of about 3 inches. The lines of the steps are curved in a similar way.

Another subtle correction is applied to the vertical lines, to counteract the apparent tendency of the building to spread outwards at the top. The columns are not truly vertical, but are set with an inclination, so that they all converge slightly towards the top. The slope could not be detected by the eye; but it was considered that, by affecting the beholder insensibly, it helped to give the building the appearance of repose and of solidity. So slight is the inclination that columns at opposite ends of the temple deviate from the vertical to the extent of not more than 2 inches; so that their axes, if produced, would meet at a point more than a mile above the ground!

The Parthenon is built of Pentelic marble from the neighbouring quarries. All the marble blocks were laid without mortar, and were worked—probably ground together—so carefully that the joints were only visible by occasional differences of colour. The columns were built up of cylindrical "drums," which appear to have been first rough-hewn, and then finished and fluted after they had been fixed in position.

Of the sculptures which adorned this wonderful building, many fine examples are now in the British Museum, where they form the chief portion of the collection known as the Elgin marbles. When Lord Elgin was ambassador to Turkey, in 1800, Athens was in the hands of the Turks, who were busily engaged in dilapidating the buildings on the Acropolis, in order to dispose of fragments to travellers. Seeing that the works of art were receiving daily injury, Lord Elgin was induced to consent to the removal of whole pieces of sculpture, which were thus saved from destruction, and eventually found a resting-place in our national museum.

The bas-reliefs in the metopes of the frieze— executed with remarkable vigour—represented the battle of the Centaurs and the Lapithæ; many of these, as well as the colossal groups of statuary which filled the pediments, were doubtless the work of Pheidias himself. Among the pediment sculptures is a noble statue of Theseus reclining. "I should say," said one of our most eminent sculptors, when giving evidence before a Committee of the House of Commons, "that the back of the Theseus was the finest thing in the world." In connection with this remark, let us remember that the statue was executed for a position some 50 or 60 feet above the eye, so that it could not be examined closely by any spectator. Moreover, the back of the statue was turned towards the wall of the building and away from the spectator; it could not, therefore, be seen by any one. This example serves to illustrate the surpassing excellence and the thoroughness which marked the work of the Greeks at their best period. Truly:

> In the elder days of art
> Builders wrought with greatest care
> Each minute and unseen part—

for we find in the Parthenon that all the work which was invisible to the spectator was as carefully and as religiously finished as that which was immediately in sight!

FIGURE 16 — *Doric Capital, showing Colour Decoration*

Colour decoration was an essential part of the Doric temple design. The Parthenon, at the time of Pericles, did not present a front of dazzling white marble, for the entire building, on the exterior as well as on the internal walls, was richly decorated with colour. The frieze, with its metopes and triglyphs, was brilliant with blue and red, the glare of the walls and columns was toned down to a pale yellow tint, and the mouldings and capitals were decorated with frets, egg and dart, and other ornaments in dark colours, so that the whole design presented an appearance of richness and gaiety, rather than of simple dignity.

PLATE VI — *The Theseum, Athens*

Time would have dealt gently with the Parthenon, if man had been more merciful. Until the seventeenth century it suffered chiefly from neglect; but in 1687 a terrible calamity overtook it, while the city was being besieged by the Venetians. Athens at that time was in possession of the Turks, who converted the Acropolis into a citadel, and stored the greater portion of their ammunition in the Parthenon. During the bombardment a Venetian shell, falling into the temple, exploded the gunpowder and wrecked a great part of the building. The Venetian commander followed up his work of destruction by breaking up, in a careless effort to remove it, a large portion of the statuary from the west front. Few attempts were then made to restore the structure, or to protect it from the damaging effects of exposure to rain and weather, and the work of decay went on speedily.

> Goodly buildings left without a roof
> Soon fall to ruin;

the unprotected parts soon began to suffer from the wet, and the iron cramps and dowels, which were largely used in the construction, rusted and caused the marble to crack and fall to pieces.

A century later, as we have seen, Lord Elgin prevented the complete destruction of many of the sculptures by removing them. This action has been keenly criticised; but if ever the end may be said to justify the means, Lord Elgin's action has been justified, for, since the removal of the most precious of the sculptures, the Acropolis has been twice bombarded (1826–1827), by the Greeks and by the Turks, with the result that the Parthenon bears the marks and scars of cannon-shot on all its faces.

Ictinus and Callicrates were the architects of this wonderful building, and to their genius was added that of the great sculptor Pheidias. The temple was in reality a stately shrine for the colossal statue of Athene, 40 feet high, of ivory and gold, the work of this artist. Much of the sculpture was also probably from his hand.

Remains of many Doric temples are to be found in different parts of Greece and of her colonies. Among these the most important are the Theseum—the best preserved of all Greek temples, in a sheltered spot below the Acropolis—the temples at Selinus and Agrigentum in Sicily, and at Paestum in Magna Græcia (South Italy), the temple of Zeus at Olympia, and of Segesta in Sicily, and that of Apollo Epicurius at Bassæ in Arcadia.

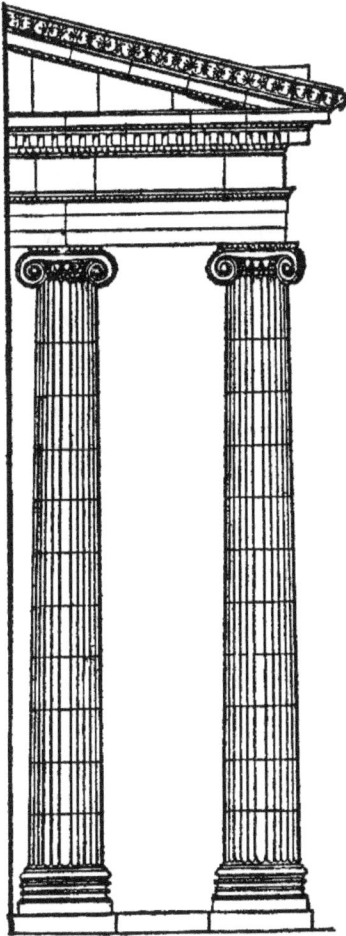

FIGURE 18 — *Ionic Order*

The Ionic order—the second of the three orders in date and importance—was developed by the Ionians or Asiatic Hellenes, who had migrated from Asia Minor. Rock-cut tombs which are found there, and the architectural remains at Persepolis, of the sixth century, B.C., possess features very similar to those which characterise the Ionic order in Greece. Some curious tombs in Lycia—accurate restorations of which may be seen in the British Museum—show the earliest works in stone of a people who had been accustomed to the use of wood, especially

49

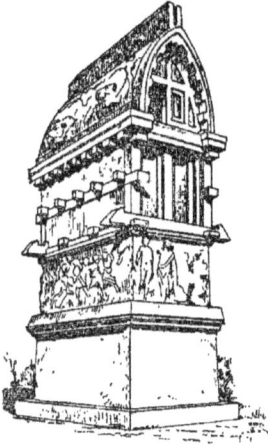

FIGURE 17 — *Stone Tomb, Lycia*

boat-building. The tombs take the form of a boat turned upside down, beams, planks and even the keel being laboriously reproduced in the stone. With such evidence before us, it is easy to understand how reminiscences of timber construction have survived in the designs of those early builders of Greece who drew their inspiration from these sources.

The Ionic order consists of a column and entablature, made up in the same way as the Doric, but differing in the details and in the general proportions. The shaft is more slender—from eight to ten diameters in height—and is surmounted by a peculiar capital which forms the most striking feature of the style. It will be noticed that the abacus is small, and that the cushion upon which it rests terminates on each side in a feature like a scroll, which is known as the "Ionic volute."

FIGURE 19 — *Ionic Capital from the Erechtheum*

The column does not spring directly from the pavement, like the Doric shaft, but stands upon a moulded base. Upon the surface of the shaft are twenty-four grooves, or flutes, rather deeper than those of the Doric order, and separated from each other by a fillet. The architrave is plain, generally with three facias; the frieze has no triglyphs, but is either plain or enriched with an uninterrupted design carved in relief. A characteristic feature in the cornice is the "dentil" course, a row of narrow blocks or tooth-like projections, which—like the Doric triglyphs—are probably reminiscences of primitive forms of construction in wood. The crowning member of the cornice was frequently enriched with carving, which took the place of the colour decoration of the Doric order.

The Ionic capital was richer and more elaborate, though less vigorous, than the Doric; it possessed, however, an awkward feature in that it was not four-sided: the front differed from the side, and at the angle of a colonnade the two-sided capital was very noticeable. It was usual, therefore, to treat the corner capital with volutes on the two exterior faces, the scrolls at the outer angle meeting one another at an angle of 45°, as shewn in the illustrations.

More numerous remains of buildings of the Ionic order exist in Asia Minor than elsewhere; but the finest and most notable example of the developed style is the Erechtheum, on the Acropolis at Athens. This building shows much variety of detail of the most refined order, and—an unusual feature in the temple designs of the Greeks—considerable irregularity of plan. This is due partly to the difference of levels, rendered necessary by the uneven site; but it is chiefly accounted for by the fact that in the one design were included shrines of several deities—Athene, Pandrosus and Erechtheus.

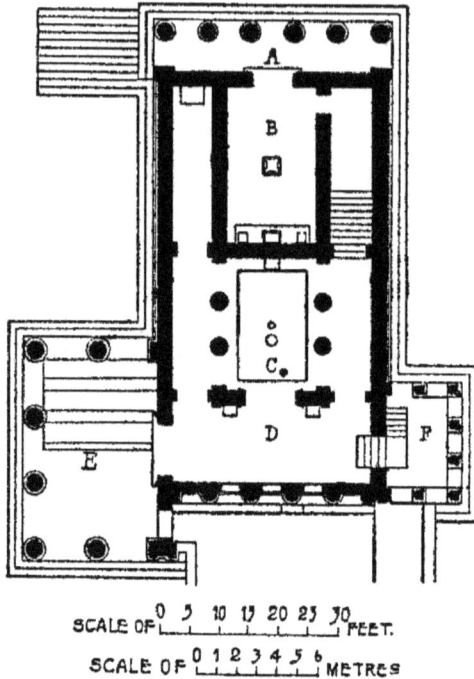

SCALE OF 0 5 10 15 20 25 30 FEET.

SCALE OF 0 1 2 3 4 5 6 METRES

FIGURE 20 — *Plan of the Erechtheum*

The Erechtheum was begun in 479 B.C., and was not completed until seventy years later, so that it was in course of erection throughout the whole of the Periclean period. A feature of the design is the little south porch, the entablature of which is supported by female figures (caryatids) in the place of columns. One of the caryatids and some examples of the carved ornament, borrowed from the Assyrian honeysuckle may be seen among the other treasures of ancient Greece in the British Museum.

The plan of this building underwent alterations in the early days of Christianity, when it was in use as a Christian church; but the wars of the seventeenth century are chiefly responsible for the mutilated condition of the temple at the present day. When Lord Elgin was in Athens at the beginning of last century, the vestibule was being used as a powder magazine, to which access could be obtained only through an opening in the wall which had been built up between the columns.

PLATE IX — *The Erechtheum, on the Acropolis, Athens*

The first building to be completed of all those now on the Acropolis was the small Ionic temple of Niké Apteros—"Wingless Victory"—which was erected about 440 B.C. This consists of a square cella with a front portico of four columns. The building appears now to be in a fair state of preservation; at one time, however, it had been completely pulled down, and its details built into a Turkish fortress or powder magazine, some of the sculptures being fixed upside down. It was rebuilt in A.D. 1836 from the old materials.

PLATE IX — *Ionic Temple of "Wingless Victory"*

Perhaps the most magnificent of all the structures ever erected by the Greeks was the Ionic temple at Ephesus, dedicated to the great "Diana of the Ephesians." This building was almost totally destroyed, possibly by an earthquake, so that the very site of it was unknown until it was discovered by an English architect, Mr. Wood, in 1871. The British Museum possesses the sculptured drum of one of the *"columnæ celatæ,"* referred to by Pliny, from whom we know that there were thirty-six of these sculptured columns, and that one of them was by a renowned artist named Scopas. The beauty of the work seems to justify the high opinion of the Greeks, who included the great temple of Ephesus among the seven wonders of the world.

Although the Doric and Ionic orders were quite distinct in their respective proportions and features, they were occasionally combined in the same building, as in the Propylæa, the noble gateway which gave access to the Acropolis at Athens. In the temple of Apollo Epicurius at Bassæ in Arcadia, designed by Ictinus, one of the architects of the Parthenon, the exterior columns were Doric, but a row of piers on each side of the interior was treated with Ionic capitals and details.

The third order—the Corinthian—was of little importance in pure Greek architecture; it appears to have been used, before the time of the Roman conquest, for comparatively small monuments. As used by the Greeks, the order resembled the Ionic in all its features, with the exception of the capital. The most graceful example is the choragic monument erected at Athens (335 B.C.), by Lysicrates, in commemoration of his victory in the choral competitions; a capital from this monument is shown in the illustration.

FIGURE 21 —
Corinthian Capital

The Corinthian capital was the great creation of the later period of Greek architecture. Possibly the first suggestions of the form were taken from the temples of the Egyptians, for there exists a striking resemblance between some of the bell-shaped capitals of Egypt and the earliest Greek examples of the Corinthian order; but to the Greek artists is due the introduction of the angle volutes and of the acanthus decoration, which combine to make the capital such an exquisite work of art.

Although the Alexandrian age was an era of great magnificence, it was, in reality, a decadent period so far as art was concerned; and after the death of Alexander (323 B.C.) architecture, never recovered its lost ground. It must be remembered that true Greek architecture ceased almost immediately after the country had come under the baneful influence of conquering Rome —*i.e.*, about the beginning of the second century B.C. Among the vast undertakings of this Roman period was the temple of the Olympian Zeus at Athens, a magnificent building of the Corinthian order, begun about 170 B.C., but not completed until 300 years later. When Sulla entered Athens with his army, he carried off several of the capitals and other portions of this temple to Rome, where they probably served the Romans as models of the Corinthian order.

Before leaving Greece, mention must be made of some buildings of which remains exist, other than temples. The largest structures were the theatres for dramatic representations, which were built frequently in an excavation of the sloping hillside, in the form shown. In the centre was an altar to Dionysus, the space around—the orchestra—being occupied by the chorus; the actors appeared on a small stage, while the audience occupied stone or marble

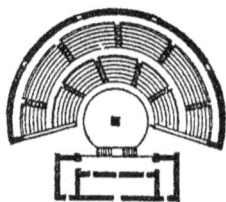

FIGURE 22 — *Plan of Greek Theatre*

56

seats, ranged in semi-circular tiers. In the theatre of Dionysus at Athens accommodation was provided for about 30,000 spectators.

The Greeks built few important tombs. The most celebrated was the mausoleum at Halicarnassus in Caria—another of the seven wonders of the world— which received its name from Mausolus, to whose memory it was erected by his wife Artemesia (*circa* 350 B.C.). This tomb was a splendid structure in the Ionic style, richly decorated with sculpture. Portions of the colossal chariot and horses which surmounted the pyramidal roof may be seen in the "Mausoleum Room" of the British Museum.

Some of the memorial stones (steles) used by the Greeks were beautifully carved, and it is interesting to notice that on many of them are found sculptured representations of the arch. Although the Greek builders were undoubtedly acquainted with the arch, they appear, so far as our knowledge goes, never to have made any practical use of it. "An arch never sleeps," says the Hindoo proverb; and the Greeks, perhaps rightly, felt that its use would detract from the simplicity and the feeling of repose to which they endeavoured to give expression in their designs.

Our knowledge of the domestic architecture of Greece is derived almost entirely from descriptions by contemporary writers, for no remains of importance have survived. The architecture and art of Pompeii savoured much of Greek influence, and the Pompeian house, described later, probably resembled in many particulars the houses of the Greeks of the earlier period.

CHAPTER III

ETRUSCAN AND ROMAN ARCHITECTURE

In dealing with the early days of Rome it is difficult to distinguish between fiction and truth, between legend and history. There was, no doubt, a good deal of human nature in the early inhabitants, which led them—after the city had gained for itself such a position as to secure the respect of all neighbouring nations—to feel that they could not have been fashioned from the same stuff as were other men. We thus find that the early traditions "mixed human things with things divine," and gave a divine origin to the eternal city. Whatever be the true story of the foundation of Rome, it appears certain that at the date assigned to it (753 B.C.) a people called Etruscans were flourishing in a highly civilised state in the immediate neighbourhood. The Etruscans were a race of foreigners, though the source from which they sprang is still debated. They were possessed of great constructive skill, and had a certain amount of artistic perception, which enabled them to exercise considerable influence upon the earlier architecture of Rome.

The Etruscan monuments which still remain in Italy consist chiefly of walls and tombs. Of the city walls we find examples at Volterra, Perugia, Cortona and elsewhere; the masonry is in some case polygonal, but is generally laid in horizontal courses, and is of the character previously referred to as "Cyclopean," the separate blocks being of an enormous size.

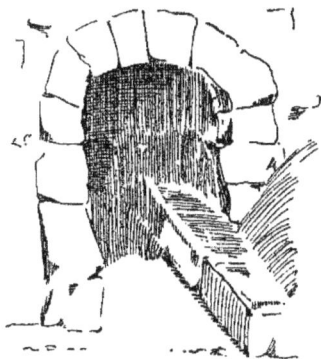

FIGURE 23 — *Earliest Roman Arch over drain in the Forum*

A true form of arch was used for the gateways in their walls, as at Volterra.

This "new" constructional principle, the arch—which had been in use long before in the East—was understood by these early builders, and until recent years the Etruscans had been credited with having introduced it to the Romans in the vaulting of the Cloaca Maxima, or great sewer in Rome.

Commendatore Boni's investigations, however, have now proved that the Cloaca was originally an uncovered drain, and that the arched vaulting, in three consecutive rings, was added by the Romans at a later date. The oldest examples of the use of the arch in Rome—far older than any other trace—may be seen in the drains which have been partly excavated in the Forum. They were tributaries of the Cloaca, and date from about 500 B.C. These arched drains formed part of an extensive system for draining the lower portion of the city, and were constructed probably in the Early

59

Republican period after the Tarquin kings had been expelled.

Etruscan tombs, of two kinds, rock-cut and structural, are found in great numbers throughout Central Italy. These contained, as a rule, one chamber only, in the form of an ordinary room; for it appears to have been the object of the constructors to make the dead tenant feel as comfortable as possible in the tomb: the walls were covered with paintings, and the chamber frequently was provided with furniture cut out of the solid rock, and with a number of utensils of use in everyday life.

The tombs have proved more permanent than the temples, for all traces of the latter have disappeared. We gather our information about them chiefly from the works of Vitruvius, a prolific, but not altogether reliable, writer of the first century A.D. In his description he tells us that the temples were of two kinds, circular and rectangular, the rectangular buildings having three cells and being devoted to the worship of three deities. So far as our records go, the most important of these was the temple of Jupiter Capitolinus, on the Capitol, begun by Tarquinius Superbus, and destroyed by fire in 80 B.C. It was adorned with many ornaments and statues of terracotta, or baked clay, of which the Etruscans made great use. These terracotta vases and ornaments are generally called Etruscan, but it must be borne in mind that the Etruscans imported large quantities of Greek vases from early times and copied them. In this and in other ways they adopted many of the Greek traditions and handed them on to the

Romans. As artists the Etruscans do not appear to have been great originators; their best work is that in which Greek myths are represented, a proof that the designers had come under the influence of the Greeks.

The architecture of the two great nations of whom the preceding chapters have treated was essentially "trabeated" (*trabs,* a beam)—*i.e.,* the openings were covered, and the superincumbent weight supported, by a flat horizontal beam or lintel. In Roman architecture, which we are about to consider, a new method of construction was employed—the principle of the arch. This soon revolutionised the art of building. The Romans received this new feature through Etruria, and quickly grasped its significance; but their architecture developed little until conquering Rome came into contact with the treasures and masterpieces of Greece.

The taste for the architecture of Greece first manifested itself in Rome in the time of the Scipios, about 200 B.C. Greece had become practically a province of Macedonia, and the victory of Paulus over the Macedonians, in 168 B.C., brought her under the influence of Rome. At a later period, when some dispute had arisen between the Achæans and the Spartans, the latter applied to Rome for help, and in response the Consul Mummius settled the question by landing in Greece and taking possession of Corinth (146 B.C.). After carrying off all the art treasures, and stipulating—in his ignorance as to their value—that if any were lost by the carriers they should be replaced by others of equal value, he set fire to the city. From this time Greece became the happy hunting-ground for works of art: the artistic treasures were freely pillaged, and their importation naturally had immense influence upon the buildings which were springing up in Rome; Greek architects also were introduced into Italy, and under these circumstances there was soon evolved that modified form of Grecian architecture known as "Roman."

We see, then, that Roman architecture was not an independent creation. Broadly speaking, it may be said to have resulted from the fusing of the styles of the Greeks and the Etruscans. Upon the architecture of the Greeks was grafted the new constructional principle, the arch, which at once enlarged its scope; but the refined, intellectual work of the Greeks was out of place in a city such as Rome was destined to be. "Rome had no time for the cultivation of the arts of peace, and as little sympathy for their gentler influences. Conquest, wealth, and consequent power were the objects of her ambition; for these she sacrificed everything, and by their means she attained a pinnacle of greatness that no nation had reached before or has since. Her arts have all the impress of this greatness, and are characterised by the same vulgar grandeur, which marks everything she did." That such an authority as Fergusson can apply the term "vulgar grandeur" to the architecture of Rome is sufficient evidence that, despite the fact that one was derived from the other, there was, between the two, a great gulf fixed.

Before dealing with the *forms* which architecture assumed in the hands of the Romans, we must say a few words about one special feature—the method of construction—which had an important bearing upon the architecture of Rome, and which was radically different from that employed by the Greeks.

The Romans, as a nation, possessed little artistic feeling; but they were an inventive, and a thoroughly practical, people, and they had an unrivalled knowledge of construction and of the use of materials. In the earliest periods of their history their buildings were constructed of solid masonry; but, before the first century B.C., the use of an artificial material came into vogue, by means of which it was possible to employ unskilled labour to a vast extent, and in the erection of every class of building; it became possible with this to build, not only on a vast scale, but at once cheaply and speedily. This material was concrete.

Concrete is an artificial conglomerate, usually made by mixing together lime or cement, sand, water and gravel or small stones. The lime, in its moist state, absorbs carbonic acid from the air and turns into carbonate of lime, or limestone, which, coming into contact with the sand and stones, sets and forms a solid mass as hard as stone. In the buildings of the Romans this material was employed far more extensively than any other; indeed, without concrete, it is safe to say that it would have been impossible for the constructors to have carried out so successfully the gigantic undertakings which, down to the present day, remain the wonder of the "eternal city."

The Roman concrete was exceptionally strong; one of its chief ingredients was a volcanic product called *pozzolana* (from Pozzuoli, where it has always been largely obtained), which, when broken up and incorporated with the lime, made a natural cement of extraordinary strength and hardness. From the first century B.C. onwards this conglomerate was extensively employed in the construction of almost every building of ancient Rome. Brickwork or masonry was used merely as a facing for the concrete mass. The boast of Augustus—recorded by Suetonius—that he found Rome brick and left it marble must, therefore, not be interpreted too literally. Under his auspices the city witnessed a period of great splendour, and marble was extensively used; many of the temples and other structures of the Augustan age were built solidly of the finest marble; but the majority of the works of this and the later periods were nothing more than concrete piles, hidden behind a veneer of marble or brickwork.

The visitor among the ruins of ancient Rome, who sees walls apparently of fine brickwork, on all sides, finds it difficult to realise that bricks were *seldom* used constructionally. Yet careful examination discloses the fact that even the thinnest walls were merely cased with bricks and filled in with concrete. The great domed Pantheon is a glaring example of a concrete mass posing as a brick structure. Externally the wall presents a solid face of brickwork, in which tiers and arcades of brick arches are arranged, as though concentrating the weight upon piers; yet the arches are, structurally, of no value whatever, for the brickwork of which they consist forms merely a casing of 4 or 5 inches, upon a solid concrete wall, 20 feet thick.

We see, than, that the constructive methods of the Romans differed in most essential points from those of the Greeks. In the Greek's building every part did the work which it was supposed to do, and which it appeared to do; never was there any attempt at deception. "Beauty is truth" formed part of his artistic creed, and he had a horror of deceit in any form. The Roman, on the other hand, openly revelled in it. Of the Roman it may be said that, as regards his architecture, he absolutely could not tell the truth—*"splendide mendax,"* he was gloriously untruthful. But, like many evil-doers, he prospered, and, by his new methods, was able to build quickly and on a grand scale.

FIGURE 24 — *Composite Capital*

"He went in," says Ruskin, "for a cheap and easy way of doing that whose difficulty was its chief honour," and was enabled, by means of his inventive genius, to enlarge greatly the scope of the architecture which had been handed down to him from the Greeks. In his hands the art was not confined to the building of temples, but was applied to new forms and adapted, in an original and daring manner, to the varied requirements of the people. Palaces, amphitheatres, baths, triumphal arches, basilicas, all on a scale of unparalleled magnificence, sprang up on every side, all presenting new problems in design and construction, which the Roman builders never shirked, but at once undertook to solve, and upon which they speedily stamped their individuality.

Out of the three orders of Greece and the Etruscan models were evolved five Roman orders:—

1. The Tuscan, a rudimentary Doric form borrowed from the Etruscans. The column was sturdy and stood upon a base; the entablature was simple and without triglyphs.

2. The Doric, which retained the triglyph. This column also had a base, and was frequently made smooth, without flutings.

3. The Ionic, very similar to the Greek order, but having a less rich capital, with smaller volutes.

4. The Corinthian, the favourite order with the Romans, in whose hands it developed into the most beautiful feature of their architecture.

5. The Composite, a poor attempt at an improvement, in which the Ionic volutes were combined with the lower portion of the Corinthian acanthus capital.

We saw that the story of architecture in Greece was told almost entirely by her temples. This was not the case in Rome; temple building was not the strong point with the Romans—though in the time of Augustus the city must have been well supplied with them—and very few remains now exist.

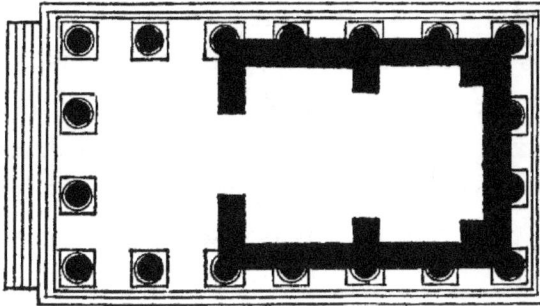

FIGURE 25 — *Plan of a Roman Temple*

The illustration shows the plan of an early temple of the Ionic order, the so-called Temple of Fortuna Virilis, the real name of which is not known. This building dates from the time of Augustus—at the end of the first century B.C. As Dr. Ashby points out, the date, in this and other cases, may be approximately ascertained by an examination of the materials used in the construction. In the early period the stone used by the Romans was a kind of tufa, called "cappellacio," and where this is found, as in the podia of the original temples of Saturn, and of Castor and Pollux, in the Forum, it seems fairly safe to attribute the date of the work to the period 550–450 B.C. A somewhat harder volcanic stone, "peperino," afterwards came into use, and at a later period, "travertine," which was more durable, and harder to work. Travertine was sparingly used before the first century B.C. In the temple of Fortuna Virilis the columns of the portico and the "engaged" columns ranged round the cell walls are of travertine.

The temple stood upon a lofty *podium,* or base, so that a flight of steps in front was required to give access to the higher floor level. The cell is short and wide, and is divided by piers which help to carry the roof. The portico is inordinately deep, and, ranging with its side columns, we see a series of "engaged" columns—*i.e.*, half-columns applied to the face of the wall as purely decorative features. From the earliest period of Roman building the column was not so important a feature in their architecture as it was with the Greeks; and, as the arch and vault came into use, it began to lose its significance, and gradually became little more than a decorative accessory, tacked on to the structural part of the design.

The details of the temple of Fortuna Virilis were thoroughly Greek in their character, and were probably executed by Greek artists; while the square cell and the deep portico are elements in the design probably due to Etruscan influence. After having been enclosed by a wall for many centuries, and incorporated into a Christian church, the portico has now been cleared, and it is proposed to conserve the temple carefully, as nearly as possible in its original state.

Greek artists were probably responsible for the details of two circular temples of this early period— the temple of Vesta at Tivoli, and the so-called temple of Vesta, or S. Maria del Sole, in Rome. In these the circular cell was surrounded by a peristyle of eighteen and twenty Corinthian columns respectively, with capitals of great beauty.

As might be expected, we find that, throughout the earlier period, when much of the designing was entrusted to Greek architects, the buildings of Rome were characterised by simplicity and purity of style;

but the increasing splendour of the empire was soon reflected in its architecture, which culminated in the reign of Augustus (27 B.C.–A.D. 14), the golden age of art and of literature. This period produced the finest, though by no means the most colossal, of the works of Rome, for Augustus employed the best of Greek sculptors, who helped to some extent to revive the glories of ancient Greek architecture. Moreover, his artists and workmen were kept busy, for during this emperor's reign were built no less than twelve temples, including those of Castor and Pollux, of Jupiter Tonans on the Capitol, and of Mars Ultor; in addition to these works he restored or helped to complete more than eighty others, and numerous secular buildings. Among the secular buildings the theatre of Marcellus, completed by Augustus B.C. 13, is a good example of the use by the Romans of the "engaged" column as a decorative feature, the orders being superimposed—Doric on the ground floor, above this the Ionic and, probably, as in the Colosseum, the Corinthian in the third storey.

Rome contains comparatively few temple remains, for a reason to be mentioned later. The most striking are the three noble Corinthian columns of the temple of Castor and Pollux, which stand up among the ruins of the Forum. This temple was rebuilt by Augustus upon the original podium, or base, of an old temple, of about 500 B.C., dedicated to the same deities. The quarries of Mount Pentelicus, near Athens, provided the marble, and Greek architects undoubtedly furnished the design and the details, which are among the finest to be found in Rome.

FIGURE 26 — *Theatre of Marcellus, Rome*

Most of the buildings of Rome were utilitarian, and even the temples appear to have been useful for purposes other than of worship. Part of the temple of Castor and Pollux, for example, served as an office for checking weights and measures, for many bronze weights exist with the inscription *"ex ad: Castor:"* showing that they had been examined and verified in the temple.

It has been mentioned that the Romans excelled in the art of construction, and that the materials used by them were of the most enduring kind. How comes it, then, that of the colossal and numerous buildings erected at this period, so few remain to-day, even in a fragmentary state?

The disappearance of the old monuments may be accounted for in two ways. Firstly, by the wanton destruction, at the hands of successive emperors, of the works of their predecessors. Each new ruler, either as a bid for popularity or in his own selfish interests, endeavoured to surpass, in magnificence, everything that had been done by those before him, and in these efforts at self-aggrandisement the existing buildings were treated with scant respect. When Nero, for example, wished to carry out an extensive scheme which he had prepared for the rebuilding of a portion of the city, he cleared a site by means of the great fire of Rome. He was thus enabled to proceed with the work, building, among other monuments, that vast and wonderful palace, the "Golden House of Nero," the most lavish, selfish and costly structure that Rome had seen—a group of buildings which, it is estimated, covered as much space as is now covered by S. Peter's, the Vatican, and the Vatican Gardens! A few years later Vespasian and Titus, each in his turn, wishing to please the people by the construction of the huge amphitheatre, the Colosseum, and of extensive baths, concluded that the site of Nero's great palace and pleasure grounds was the most eligible for the purpose. Without delay, down came a great part of the Golden House, in order to provide a space for the new buildings. Trajan completed its destruction later by the erection of his immense baths, almost upon the very site of the Golden House, so that it is now difficult to trace even the vestiges of Nero's stupendous work.

Secondly, as Christianity spread in Rome, the temples—representing the old Pagan religion—were not only neglected, but were, in many instances, destroyed, the materials being reused in the construction of new buildings. This state of affairs lasted for centuries. The marble temple of Castor and Pollux, to take an example, was, during this period, almost carried away piecemeal. Michael Angelo used a portion of one column for the pedestal upon which was set the equestrian statue of Marcus Aurelius; another portion was made into the marble statue of Jonah in the church of S. Maria del Popolo. The great Basilica Julia, in the Forum, another Augustan building, was used as a marble quarry in the Middle Ages; the greater part of the structure was carried away for building purposes, and the remainder was burnt into lime on the spot. In the course of some excavations, three lime-kilns were found in this building.

Vandalism has often gone hand in hand with civilisation. "The excavators of the sixteenth century have done more harm to the antiquities," says Lanciani, "than all the barbarians of the Middle Ages." When Charles V visited Rome in 1536, the Pope, wishing to honour him as the avenger of Christianity, arranged that he should pass successively beneath the triumphal arches of Titus, Constantine and Severus. "With this object," says Rabelais, who was an eye-witness, "they demolished more than 200 houses and razed three or four churches level with the ground."

Small wonder, then, that for the finest example of a typical Roman temple we have to go out of Rome, and indeed out of Italy, to the Maison Carrée, at Nîmes, in France, erected during the reign of Hadrian (A.D. 117–138). This temple differs very little, in the arrangement of its parts, from the temple of Fortuna Virilis, to which we have previously referred. In each case the edifice rests upon a raised podium, requiring a flight of steps in the front for access to the floor. The portico is deep in proportion to its width, and the walls of the cell are decorated with engaged columns, which range with the free columns of the portico.

FIGURE 27 — *Maison Carrée, Nîmes*

After the Augustan ages, as wealth continued to pour into Rome, the magnificence of the city increased, for the Romans' method was, in the words of Pliny, "to take everywhere whatever they thought worth taking," and the buildings of the period were the natural outcome of the increasing licence and prodigality of the times. A typical building was the Flavian amphitheatre, better known, from its vast proportions, as the Colosseum, begun by the first of the Flavian emperors, Vespasian, in A.D. 70.

For the Greeks' form of amusement—dramatic representation—the Romans cared little; but they were passionately fond of gladiatorial shows and contests. Wherever a Roman settlement existed—in Britain, in Gaul, or in the mother country—traces are found of these amphitheatres. As would be expected, Rome claimed the most gigantic of them all.

The Colosseum was built in the form of a vast ellipse, 610 feet long, 510 feet wide, and 180 feet high. In the centre, communicating with the wild beasts' dens, was the arena in which the gladiatorial contests and spectacles were held; around this, rows of seats, rising in tiers, gave accommodation to 80,000 spectators, who were partially protected from the sun's rays by a huge awning. The structure was built almost entirely of concrete, faced with stone, and was skilfully planned to allow the whole audience a clear view of the arena. On the exterior the three lower stories formed continuous arcades of semi-circular arched openings, eighty in number. In front of the piers which separated the openings were engaged columns used, after the Roman manner, as decorative accessories; the Tuscan order in the lowest storey, the Ionic in the second, and the Corinthian in the third. The fourth storey, consisting of an almost unbroken wall divided by Corinthian pilasters, was added, or rebuilt, in the third century. It served to support the masts, fixed round the building in a series of corbels, from which the great awning was stretched.

The vast scale upon which the Colosseum is built renders it one of the most imposing ruins of the world; but, apart from its skilful construction, it had little architectural merit. The exterior, with its endless repetition of arches and useless columns, was monotonous. Such a building, persistently devoted to the most brutal contests, was a typical product of Roman civilisation. For more than 300 years it was the scene of bloody contests of gladiators and prisoners, and echoed with the multitude's

> loud-roared applause
> As man was slaughtered by his fellow-man,

until the year A.D. 403, when the better feeling of the people was aroused by the self-sacrifice of a monk named Telemachus. His story is the one redeeming feature in the long history of the Colosseum. In order to protest against the wanton cruelty, the monk rushed on to the arena, and fell a victim to the rage of the spectators; but the moral effect was such that human slaughter in the contests was discontinued.

Huge as was the Colosseum, there was another building devoted to Roman "sports"—the Circus Maximus—which far surpassed it. No vast building in Rome has vanished so completely as has this great circus; from its mass, no doubt, "palaces, half cities, have been reared," for almost every vestige has disappeared, so that its very name is hardly recalled by the visitor to the sights of modern Rome. From comparatively small beginnings in the time of the Tarquins, the Circus Maximus gradually developed until, after its restoration by the Emperor Claudius, it held, according to Pliny, no less than 250,000 spectators. Additional splendour was added by Trajan, under whom the vast building was wholly covered, inside and out, with white marble, relieved with brilliant mosaics, oriental marble columns and statuary. "It must then," says Professor Middleton, "from its crowd of works of art, its immense size, and the splendour of its materials, have been, on the whole, the most magnificent building in the world." In the fourth century it covered an area of more than four times that of the Colosseum, and accommodated—according to records—the almost incredible number of 485,000 spectators.

Triumphal arches, in commemoration of victories, were striking features in Roman design. In the second century A.D. the city contained no less than thirty-eight. Of the few that remain, the arch of Titus, erected A.D. 71–80, to commemorate the conquest of Jerusalem, is best known for its fine proportion and the excellence of its details. The arch of Septimius Severus (A.D. 203), in the Forum, and that of Constantine (A.D. 330), are left as examples of the later work. The latter, though built at a period when Roman art was most degraded, contains some excellent sculptures and details. This is explained by the fact that the marble columns and entablatures, the sculptured panels (representing Trajan's victories), and the colossal statues of Dacian captives, are of much earlier date, for they were taken from the arch and forum of Trajan—another illustration of the ruthless manner in which the emperors destroyed the works of their predecessors. At a later date one of the fine columns of black Numidian marble was carried off for use in the church of S. John Lateran, where it now stands.

FIGURE 28 — *Arch of Constantine*

The upper storey (called the *attic*), which—as in the arch of Constantine—was frequently added above the main cornice, is a feature of Roman architecture. The purely decorative purpose of the columns is shown by the fact that, in order to give them the appearance of supporting something it has been necessary to break out the cornice and entablature over each capital. In this special case, the great statues they support afford an excuse for the presence of the columns; but in many examples of Roman work the uselessness of the column is too apparent.

In adapting the Greek orders to an arched system of construction, the Romans fell into some strange errors. They appeared not to understand that the arch *took the place* of the architrave as the supporting member; it seemed to them that the column was not complete without its entablature, so that it became the custom to insert a square piece of entablature between the column and the arch or vault—an illogical piece of construction, which was revived by the builders of the Renaissance, and is in evidence in the work of the present day.

FIGURE 29 — *Roman Entablature (Baths of Diocletian)*

Under the Flavian emperors, towards the end of the first century, art in Rome was at a very low ebb, although buildings of colossal extent were erected by these rulers to please the taste and catch the votes of the populace. Under Hadrian, however (A.D. 117–138), there was a great revival of taste, not in Rome only, but in the provinces, and especially at Athens, where the emperor rebuilt part of the city, and completed the great temple of Jupiter Olympius, begun 300 years before.

To Hadrian's time belongs the great circular Pantheon, one of the noblest of all buildings of ancient

Rome, built upon the site of an earlier rectangular temple erected by Agrippa; the portico was, indeed, rebuilt from the materials of the older temple, and has Agrippa's inscription upon its frieze. The great dome—of almost exactly the same diameter as S. Peter's, though apparently much vaster—is composed partly of concrete and partly of what may almost be called reinforced concrete—bands of bricks laid horizontally between wide layers of cement. It affords a striking illustration of the value of concrete to a nation of builders like the Romans. The construction of a dome of such magnitude—but built up of separate blocks of masonry, exerting lateral thrusts—was a problem which was to exercise the minds of master-builders many hundreds of years later. In a concrete structure, however, such as the Pantheon, the dome and vaults exercise no lateral thrust; the concrete becomes consolidated into a rigid mass, which rests upon the walls like a solid lid. This is a point which should be thoroughly grasped by the student, for it enables him to understand why the Romans, in constructing their huge vaulted roofs, were able to dispense with the buttress—so necessary to the builders of later days—and to carry their massive vaulting upon simple walls.

Light was admitted to the Pantheon in an impressive manner by means of a circular opening, 30 feet in diameter, at the top of the dome. "There is," says Fergusson, "a grandeur and a simplicity in the proportions of this great temple that render it still one of the very finest and most sublime interiors in the world. It possesses, moreover, one other element of

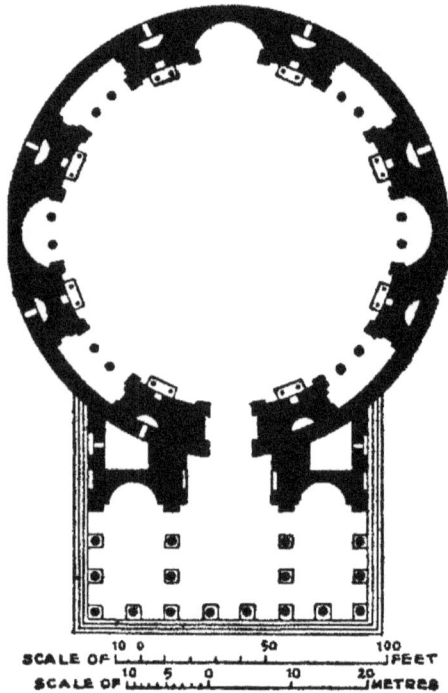

FIGURE 30 — *Plan of Pantheon*

architectural sublimity in having a single window, and that placed high up in the building. I know of no other temples which possess this feature, except the great rock-cut Buddhist basilicas of India. That one great eye opening upon heaven is by far the noblest conception for lighting a building to be found in Europe."

The interior of the dome is "coffered"—*i.e.,* divided into deep panels, which were originally gilt. The exterior is less imposing, though, in its best days, when the lower portion of the walls was encased in marble, the pediment and attic filled with bronze statuary, and the roof covered with bronze gilt tiles, few buildings surpassed the Pantheon in magnificence.

Space will permit only of a passing reference to the *thermæ,* or colossal baths, which were, at one period, the most conspicuous feature of Roman architecture, and the most remarkable of all buildings in magnitude and splendour. These vast structures, which comprised public and private baths of all kinds, gymnasia, libraries, theatres, lecture-halls, all fitted up more lavishly than the most luxurious of modern clubs, were built simply as bribes by the emperors, one after the other, to secure the vote and favour of the people. The earlier baths—of Agrippa, Nero, Vespasian, Trajan, and others—have almost entirely disappeared; two only, of the later emperors, remain in a sufficiently perfect condition to allow a restoration to be made with any degree of certainty.

The baths of Caracalla (A.D. 211), covered a site a little less than a quarter of a mile square, and now form the most extensive mass of ruins in Rome, though they suffered much, in the sixteenth century, at the hands of Pope Paul III, who carried off vast quantities of the material for use in the construction of the Farnese Palace.

The baths of Diocletian, built a century later, were probably still vaster; the grand hall, 340 feet long— restored by Michael Angelo, but still retaining the original columns and vaulting—now forms the church of S. Maria degli Angeli.

We have made no mention yet of another type of building in Rome, which was destined to exert very considerable influence upon the architecture of succeeding ages. Rome was a great commercial centre, and the public business of the city, commercial and judicial, occupied the attention of the people far more than did their religious affairs. This business was transacted in large, lofty buildings called *basilicas*, which served the purpose of halls of justice as well as commercial exchanges. A special interest attaches to them from the fact that they served as models for the first places of worship built by the early Christians of Rome, and that they thus became the recognised type for churches built for Christian worship. Compared with other Roman structures, they were slightly built; and as the materials of the old basilican halls were found to be exceedingly useful for the construction of the new churches, extensive use was made of these ancient buildings for this purpose, so that few remains of the old basilicas of pagan Rome exist. The fate of the great Basilica Julia, in the Forum, has already been referred to; the remains of the Basilica Ulpia, erected by Trajan (A.D. 115), may still be seen in Trajan's forum, adjoining his column.

FIGURE 31 — *Plan of Basilica Ulpia*

In the plan of this building we have a great hall, 360 feet long by 180 feet wide, consisting of a wide, lofty central nave, flanked by double aisles with lower roofs. At the end is a semicircular recess, or apse, called the tribune, round which, upon a raised dais, were the seats for the magistrates, or assessors, the central seat, at a higher level than the others, being set apart for the chief magistrate who presided over the business.

The roof of the basilica was usually of wood, with the nave portion considerably higher than that over the aisles, so as to allow the introduction of a clerestory wall and windows above the columns. In the Ulpian basilica the nave was probably open and only the side aisles roofed.

It was not until the time of Constantine that vaulted construction was applied to the basilicas. This emperor completed the building, which had been begun by Maxentius near the Roman forum, now called the basilica of Constantine (Plate XI, p. 84). In front of this hall was a narthex, or porch—extending the whole width of the building—which gave access to the main entrance, while a side entrance led from the Via Sacra. Opposite each doorway was an apse for the accommodation of the magisterial bench. The one existing aisle, spanned by three massive concrete vaults, affords the visitor of the present day an excellent opportunity for studying the Roman methods of building, and also shows a very early example of concrete "re-inforced" with ribs of tiles. The only known instance of metal being used to re-inforce concrete is in the baths of Caracalla.

PLATE XI — *Basilica of Constantine, Rome*

Of the private houses or homes of the Romans there are few remains in Rome itself. During the last years of the Republic, however, the Palatine was a favourite place of residence of the great Romans. Cicero, Catiline and Hortensius lived there; but few traces of houses remain, with the exception of the house of Hortensius, or "House of Livia," as it has been usually called. This house was bought by Augustus and used for a time as a meeting place of the Senate. It owes its preservation probably to the respect in which the founder of the Empire was always held. The painted decoration of the house belongs to his period.

Good examples of domestic architecture are found in the towns of Pompeii and Herculaneum, which were destroyed—or, rather, buried—by the eruption of Vesuvius in A.D. 79. But a great number of the people were forced to live in flats, and for typical houses of this kind we must go to Ostia, the ancient port and emporium of Rome, where may be seen the remains of many flats of the period. These were well-planned, and were often of three or four storeys, with a separate entrance and staircase for each floor. Recent excavations there have shown that in some of the best houses of the old Romans, hydraulic lifts were fitted and complete arrangements provided for heating and the supply of hot water.

In the Pompeian house many of the rooms facing the street, as in the house of Pansa (marked S), were used as shops, and were quite separate from the mansion. The front door opened directly from the street into a small lobby (L), which led to the *atrium*—a courtyard

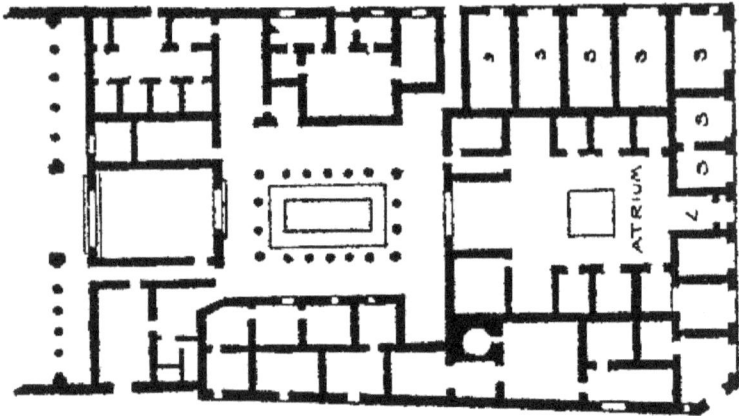

FIGURE 32 — *Plan of the House of Pansa*

roofed over round the sides, but open to the sky in the centre. Under this central opening was a tank, the *compluvium,* which collected the rain water. Three rooms at the end of the court, the *tablinum* and the *alœ,* were used for storing the family archives. By the side of these apartments a passage led to the more private portion of the house. Here, we find, is a larger court, uncovered in the centre as before—the *peristylium*— the roof of which was supported, in the houses of the wealthy, by rows of columns (peristyles) of the finest marble. Leading off this is the dining-room (*triclinium*), a most important room in the house of the old Roman, who sometimes had two or three, so that he could vary the aspect according to the time of the year and the state of his digestion. The other family rooms were grouped round the peristyle, while the bakery, kitchen and offices completed the establishment.

The walls of the interior were decorated with marble slabs or with fantastic paintings, "Pompeian decoration," as it is called, from the fact that we have been made familiar with it from the well-preserved walls of Pompeii, though it was probably in general use among the Romans of the period. In this decorative scheme the wall-spaces were divided into darkly coloured panels by means of attenuated painted columns; in the centre of the panels graceful and highly finished human figures or architectural and perspective views were introduced. Frequently the plinth, or lower portion of the wall, was painted a very dark colour, almost black; above this, a deep red or brown was used, occasionally blue or yellow. The figure treatment and the general system of decoration suggest a Greek origin: it is probable— though the theory must be always speculative—that the houses of the Romans, as preserved to us at Pompeii, were in all general features very similar to those of the Greeks of the earlier period. Mr. Petrie's remarkable discoveries in Egypt, however, enable us to trace back the Pompeian plan to a still more remote date, for his excavations of the village of Kahun, built for the overseers and the workmen of the Illahun Pyramid, have disclosed the plans of a number of large houses arranged upon a plan strikingly similar to those of Pompeii.

We have now completed the short story of the two great styles—Greek and Roman—comprising what is known as "classical architecture." The histories of the two are inseparable, yet they differ strangely—the refined, truthful, exquisitely proportioned work of the Greeks, and the vast, magnificent, daring undertakings of the Romans. "The Greek," says Ruskin, "rules over the arts to this day, and will for ever, because he sought not for beauty, not first for passion, or for invention, but for Rightness." For this quality in their architecture the Romans cared not a rap; nor was their national life, which their architecture reflected, overburdened with the sense of it. While they were under the influence of Greece, before vice and the love of luxury had fully possessed the people, Roman art progressed. But as wealth poured into Rome, and her people lived dissolutely upon the spoils of the conquered nations, her architecture became more and more debased, and its story differed little from that of Rome itself:

> First freedom, and then glory—when that fails,
> Wealth, vice, corruption—barbarism at last.

CHAPTER IV

EARLY CHRISTIAN ARCHITECTURE

DURING the first three centuries of the Christian era the new religion, though despised and discredited, had been slowly gaining ground, in the face of enormous difficulties. Rome, as we have seen, was given over to the worst kind of licence and debauchery. The old pagan religion was entirely played out; the majority of the people thought nothing about religion, pagan or otherwise; while, of those who took the trouble to think at all, few had any faith in the old creeds. The monumental undertakings of the emperors, whether sacred or secular, were not prompted by piety or by the spirit of reverence; and among the people the more thoughtful and intellectual viewed the prevailing licentiousness and prodigality with apprehension:—

> On that hard pagan world disgust
> And secret loathing fell,

and men's minds were gradually being prepared for the great upheaval.

On the other hand, it must be remembered that the Christian doctrines were not such as would be cordially welcomed by the vast majority among the pleasure-loving Romans, and the new worship had, in consequence, to be carried on in secret; hence the earliest forms of art which it developed were sepulchral, consisting of the memorials and symbols of the faith found in the Catacombs.

The religion had little direct influence upon architecture until it was officially recognised by the Emperor Constantine in the year 328; but no sooner had it taken its position as a State religion than the strength of the movement became apparent, and there sprang up on all sides a demand for places of Christian worship. The old temples were not suitable for the accommodation of large congregations, and there was, perhaps, some hesitation about making use of buildings which had been specially designed for pagan worship. In their dilemma the early Christian builders turned to the great halls of commerce, the basilicas, and found what they were wanting. The interior arrangements of the basilica suited the requirements of the new worship, and, as builders with inventive genius were scarce in Rome at the time, it thus came about that the first Christian churches were built in direct imitation of these great houses of assembly. As we shall see in succeeding chapters, this model, once adopted, was never departed from. There was no lack of materials, for the city was filled with buildings upon which all kinds of extravagance had been lavished, and which were now beginning to fall into disrepute and neglect. Columns and rich capitals, marble linings, architraves and ornaments were appropriated wholesale, and applied to new purposes, and while pagan Rome suffered, Christian basilicas sprang up in all directions with astonishing rapidity.

At the present day there is no Christian building in Rome dating from the time of Constantine. The church of S. John Lateran was built in his reign, but all trace of its early work has disappeared under the changes of later centuries. Perhaps the most beautiful of all the Christian basilicas of the time was that of S. Paul Outside the Walls, built by Theodosius in 386. Unfortunately, a great portion was destroyed by fire in 1821, but it was rebuilt with much of its former splendour—"the noblest interior in Europe, and nobly and faithfully restored," it is called by Ruskin, who seldom sang the praises of the restorer. The sketch plan of the basilica shows how closely the Christian building follows the line of its pagan prototype.

FIGURE 33 — *Cloister S. Paul Outside the Walls, Rome*

In front of the church was an arcaded porch, or *narthex,* which in the earlier buildings was usually built as one side of a square, so as to form an open courtyard. This courtyard, or atrium, occupied a considerable area, and gradually tended to disappear as space in the city became more valuable. Examples may still be seen in the churches of S. Clemente in Rome (FIGURE 36) and S. Ambrogio in Milan.

The semi-circular apse, in the basilica of the early Christians, occupied the central portion of the wall opposite the entrance, and accommodated the bishop and the chief officers. The clergy officiated in the raised space before the apse, in front of which was the altar. As the ritual became more elaborate, in order to increase the accommodation, rudimentary transepts were sometimes formed—as in the basilica of S. Paul— by slightly widening the building at this part. The choir and others who were assisting at the service required a considerable space, and for their use a portion of the nave, in front of the altar, was enclosed by a low marble screen or a railing; pulpits, or "ambos," were arranged on each side of this reserve. In the remaining portion of the nave, or in the aisles, sat the faithful who had been baptised, for no others were admitted within the church. Probationers and other worshippers were allowed only in the narthex or in the atrium.

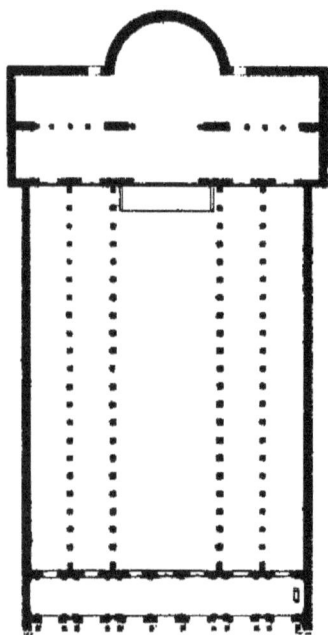

FIGURE 34 — *Plan of S. Paul Outside the Walls.*

We see, then, in these first efforts of the early Christians, the embryo plan, or arrangement of parts, which afterwards developed into the typical mediæval cathedral plan. The division into nave and aisles—borrowed from the pagan basilica—is the treatment most widely adopted in buildings for Christian worship at the present day. The influence of the narthex may be traced in many cathedral plans, as at Westminster Abbey and Durham, where the westernmost bay is wider and its piers different in character from those of the remainder of the nave. In the early basilicas, too, we see foreshadowed the transept and the resulting cruciform plan of later cathedrals. To meet the demand for extra accommodation, rudimentary transepts were formed by an extension of the space between the apse and the end of the nave: this was kept free from columns and from all other obstructions, in order that the officiating clergy might not be hampered in the administration of the ritual.

The builders of this period possessed little inventive genius, nor did they concern themselves about architectural effect. The generally accepted type of building, borrowed from their pagan forebears, satisfied them, and was never changed unless the exigencies of the service demanded an alteration. So long as the apse sufficed for the accommodation of the limited number of higher officers for whose use it was reserved, it was retained in its primitive form, though made gloriously brilliant by an incrustation of mosaic. But as the office of the clergy assumed greater importance, and the ritual grew more exclusive and elaborate, it became necessary to enlarge the space. The apse was, therefore, gradually lengthened in accordance with the requirements for increased accommodation, until it developed at last into the choir of the mediæval church.

We have seen that the transepts, in the early stage of their existence, served only a utilitarian purpose. At a later period, however, more consideration was given to their architectural effect, as regards both the exterior and the interior. It was noted that the transeptal projections formed a useful break in the long, monotonous line of the building; moreover, in England, especially, the great central tower—the dominant feature of our mediæval cathedral design—springing from the intersection of the nave and the cross walls, required the abutment of the transepts in order to support its great weight. This led to the fuller development of the transepts for architectural and structural reasons. The cruciform church-plan appears, then, to have first arisen from a combination of accidental circumstances, though it was afterwards invested with a symbolical meaning, as representing the form of the cross.

The atrium, or fore-court, which some of the early basilican churches possessed, was possibly suggested by the similar feature in the Roman house. It helped to shut off the sacred building from the outer world, and, as we have said, provided accommodation for those of the worshippers who were not fully qualified to attend the service within the building. In cathedrals of later date the atrium still survives in the cloister, though its position has been changed. The two ambos of the basilica are represented in modern churches by the reading-desk and the pulpit, situated on either side of the choir.

In almost every feature, then, the Gothic cathedral plan of mediæval times represents the natural development of the old basilican church of the early Christians. One change should be mentioned, which has been made in the position of the altar and of the bishop's seat. The early Christian basilicas resembled their prototypes, as the bishop occupied the seat in the centre of the apse, which had formerly been assigned to the chief magistrate; this seat became, in fact, the bishop's throne, and was raised up above the level of the seats of the surrounding clergy, the altar, meanwhile, being placed centrally in front of the apse. In a few

FIGURE 35 — *Development of Basilica*

of the later churches this arrangement is still adhered to, as in S. Peter's at Rome, where the Pope's throne is situated in the middle of the apse, and the high altar occupies a position in front, under the centre of the great dome. In western cathedrals generally, however, the positions have been changed: the altar occupies a central position against the wall of the apse, and the bishop is accommodated elsewhere at the *side* of the choir.

Great reverence was paid by the early Christians to the remains of the saint to whom the church was dedicated, whose baptistery and font—usually a circular or polygonal building —adjoined the basilica. At a later period the shrine was placed under the altar, in the apse. In due course the belief in the efficacy of various saints led to the erection of secondary altars; and, the apse being recognised as the natural position for an altar, it became customary to build apsidal recesses for its accommodation. At first the secondary apses were added on either side of the central recess, but as the main apse extended and developed into the choir, occupying the full width of the building, the apsidal chapels were either relegated to the transepts or were ranged round the main central apse, an arrangement which became a special feature of French cathedral architecture.

The exterior of the basilica was treated in the simplest manner possible, with no attempt at architectural embellishment, while the interior depended upon the accessories for its beauty, rather than upon architectural form. The walls inside were rich with veined marbles, and brilliant with mosaic—the most permanent of all forms of decoration, for the golden mosaics of these early basilicas are still undimmed after the lapse of centuries. The apse and the wall space over its arch— the triumphal arch, as it was called—were especially rich with pictures worked in these small glass cubes, many of them almost childish in drawing, but all finely decorative.

Inlaid marbles were used for the floor, in geometric patterns, forming a sort of mosaic known as *opus Alexandrinum*—a fine specimen of which may be seen in our own country in the presbytery of Westminster Abbey. In many of the buildings is found an odd mixture of columns and capitals, collected from the older buildings of pagan Rome; plain and fluted shafts are placed side by side, Ionic columns contrasting with Corinthian, as in S. John Lateran, Corinthian with Doric; small capitals upon large columns, shafts of different lengths raised upon bases of unequal heights, and so on; for, in Ruskin's words, "the architect of a Romanesque basilica gathered his columns and capitals where he could find them, as an ant picks up sticks"—a heterogeneous collection, sometimes, built up with little intelligent skill, guilty of little architectural style, but brimful of history!

Restoration in later days has destroyed much of the interest, historical and otherwise, of these early basilicas, Sta. Maria Maggiore, though to some extent restored in the Renaissance period, when the panelled ceiling was added, still retains almost its original aspect, and affords the best example of an old Christian basilica in Rome. It is a three-aisled building in the form of a long rectangle, with the usual apse, and with a narthex extending along the whole of the front. The nave is flanked by five colonnades of Ionic columns, all the columns being, in this case, of one design. Above the columns the clerestory wall is carried upon an architrave, not upon a series of arches, as in S. Paul Outside the Walls, S. Clemente, and most of the other basilicas. S. Clemente, although rebuilt in the eleventh century, retains its old plan, with the choir enclosure, ambos and baldaquin in a good state of preservation, and a large atrium or forecourt.

During the fifth and sixth centuries the city of Ravenna, on the Adriatic coast, was second only to the old capital in importance, and witnessed the erection of churches which were hardly inferior to the finest which Rome herself possessed. The principal of these— the ancient cathedral of Ravenna— was destroyed in the last century to make way for a modern building; but, of the other churches, two of the basilican type of especial interest have been preserved—S. Apollinare Nuovo (A.D. 525), and S. Apollinare in Classe (A.D. 549), the latter situated in what was formerly the port, at a distance of three miles from the city.

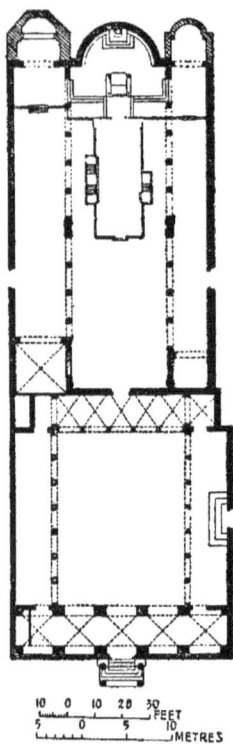

FIGURE 36 — *Plan of S. Clemente, Rome*

The plan of these churches is similar to that of the Roman basilicas; but as Ravenna differed from Rome in possessing few pagan temples which might be despoiled for the adornment of the new buildings, it was necessary that all the details required in the basilicas should be specially worked for the places they were to

FIGURE 37 — *S. Clemente, Rome*

occupy. Thus in Ravenna one does not meet with the incongruous medley which characterised many of the Christian basilicas of Rome. The features of classical Rome were imitated, but they were subjected to new influences, and the task of adapting them to the new requirements called forth the best inventive powers of the architects.

A feature of special interest in the Ravenna churches is the *dosseret*, or impost block, in shape like an inverted pyramid, which was interposed between the capital and the springing of the arches—a form in common use with the architects of Byzantium. Ravenna at this period carried on an extensive trade with Byzantium, and was

FIGURE 38 —
Capital with dosseret, Ravenna

99

subjugated by the Byzantine Emperor Justinian in 537. Thus the presence of oriental details in the buildings can be readily accounted for. But, in addition to these details, there are found in Ravenna entire buildings— to which reference must now be made—constructed upon a plan essentially different from the basilican type. To this style the name of Byzantine has been given, since it originated from the new Eastern capital which Constantine founded at Byzantium.

The basilican form of church was adopted in all parts of Italy, and continued to be built for many centuries with but slight modifications of the interior. More changes were made externally, for, instead of the barn-like treatment which characterised the early basilicas, we find somewhat elaborate exterior decorations of marble veneer, as at S. Miniato in Florence, or picturesque wall arches as at Pisa, Lucca and Pistoja.

BYZANTINE ARCHITECTURE.—We must now return to notice the new development which was taking place while the Christians were erecting their first basilicas in Rome. Intelligent builders in that city were scarce, and architectural styles had become corrupted—a result to which the prevailing practice of destroying ancient monuments and transferring their materials to new buildings for reuse had largely contributed. But, while Rome was languishing, a new era was beginning to dawn for ancient Byzantium, to which Constantine transferred the seat of the empire in the fourth century. Under him the new capital—situated upon the highway of commerce between East and West—grew rapidly in importance. Architecture kept pace with the other developments, but it was carried out under new conditions. Some of the fundamental principles of construction were adopted from Rome; moreover, Constantine, with the view of lowering the importance of the old capital as a rival, carried off from the principal Roman buildings numbers of columns, capitals and such other architectural ornaments as could be reused in his Byzantine undertakings; but many of his architects, as well as the majority of the artisans he employed, were Greeks or of Greek descent, hailing from Asia Minor and the East. Byzantium, too, by its trade was brought into direct contact with other nations of the far East, so that there sprang up an oriental taste for brilliance and rich colour decoration, which at once manifested itself in the architecture.

The divergence from the Roman style is readily observable in the church plan. The simple, rectangular, three-aisled basilica was almost unknown in Byzantium, where its place was taken by a square, vaulted building. In approaching a typical Byzantine church, such as that of Hagia Sophia at Constantinople, or S. Mark's, Venice, the spectator's eye is attracted by the broken sky-line formed by a series of roof-domes, so different from the uninterrupted line of the old basilica roof. The dome, in fact, was the distinguishing feature of Byzantine architecture; and its constant use, for the purpose of roofing over the

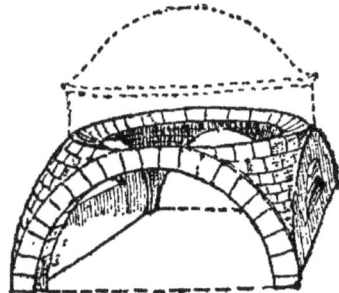

FIGURE 39 — *Diagram*

PLATE X — *Interior of S. Sophia, Constantinople*

spaces, had much to do with the radical change of plan from the long rectangle to the square, or Greek-cross form of building.

The Byzantine dome was carried upon four arches enclosing a square, as shown in the diagram on p. 101, the triangular spaces between the circular dome and the arches being filled in with "pendentives," upon which the dome really rests. It will be seen that each course of masonry forming the pendentives is kept in position by reason of its convexity, so that the dome (shown by the dotted lines) rests securely upon the upper course, at the level of the crown of the arches—*i.e.* upon the four pendentives.

The most magnificent example of the Byzantine style is the great church at Constantinople, built during the reign of Justinian, by Anthemius of Tralles and Isidorus of Miletus, A.D. 532–538, and dedicated to Hagia Sophia, the Holy Wisdom, more commonly called the church of S. Sophia (PLATE X, opposite). The main building is roofed over by a great central dome, 107 feet in diameter, lighted by a ring of forty small arched windows ranged round the base. The spaces on the east and west are covered by half-domes, which in turn cover semi-circular apses. Both the half-domes and the apses are lighted by rings of windows, for upon these roof-openings the whole interior largely depends for light. The weight of the roof is almost entirely carried upon the massive piers which divide the aisles into three bays; so that the whole of the nave, measuring more than 200 feet in length and 100 feet in breadth, is unobstructed by columns or piers of any kind. This result was obtained by the development, under Greek influence, of the possibilities of the arch as a structural principle, to an extent unknown among the builders of imperial Rome.

The vast nave, roofed over with dome upon dome, culminating in the great central vault; the numerous windows, at all heights, vying with the arcades of arches to confuse the eye and thus enlarge the apparent size of the great hall; the precious marble sheathings of the walls, the rich and delicately carved capitals, and the wonder and wealth of the mosaics, undimmed by the lapse of centuries, with which the vaults are incrusted,—these all combine to make the interior of this vast building one of the most impressive and most harmonious of the triumphs of architecture.

The many influences which were at work on Byzantine architecture resulted in a great variety of plans. At Ravenna, for example, where the art of Rome mingled with that of Byzantium, we have seen that in some of the basilicas—*e.g.,* S. Apollinare in Classe and S. Apollinare Nuovo—the Roman type of building was clothed with details of Oriental character. But other churches differed radically from these. The baptistery of San Giovanni, the surviving portion of a basilica of the fifth century, shows a simple octagonal plan. Octagonal also, but more complicated, is the exquisite church of S. Vitale, where the central dome is carried upon eight piers, between each of which is a semi-circular niche or apse; around these is carried an aisle bounded by octagonal walls. In the mosaic churches of Sicily of the twelfth century the Greek artists of Byzantium have left us priceless legacies: the little Martorana Chapel and the Capella Palatina at Palermo, and, in part, the Cathedral of Monreale.

Little attention was paid to the architectural treatment of the exteriors; but the richness of the interiors of the churches of the Byzantine style gives them an interest and a beauty hardly surpassed by buildings of any age. The vaulted system of construction which was adopted produced unbroken expanses of wall and ceiling, which were disturbed very little by projections or mouldings— smooth surfaces upon which a decorative effect was gained by means of mosaics. Figure-sculpture and painting had become almost lost arts at this time, and the drawings of the mosaic-workers were rudely simple; but the materials with which the artists worked their symbolical glass-pictures atoned for much that was lacking in the design, and imparted marvellous beauty and splendour to the simple lines of the architecture. The custom—which originated in Rome—of incrusting the lower walls and the piers with precious marbles, and of enriching the floors with elaborate marble pavements of *opus Alexandrinum,* contributed to the general effect of splendour and brilliance.

There was much rich carving also of the marble surfaces. The undersides of the arches and the spandrils, or triangular spaces between them, were covered with delicately incised patterns; the capitals of the columns were exquisitely carved in crisp low relief, with symbolical emblems, leaf-decoration, etc., and with incised basket-work patterns. Sometimes the volutes and other features of the classical architecture of Rome were suggested, but the general form was similar to the illustration on p. 99.

Above the capital was the impost-block, or *dosseret,* which we noticed at Ravenna—a very familiar feature in Byzantine work, and probably a reminiscence of the fragmentary entablature of the architecture of the Romans.

Like the Parthenon in the midst of the architecture of Greece, the great church of S. Sophia remains unrivalled by any building of its class (PLATE X, p. 102). Further west, the most beautiful result of the influence of Byzantium is the church of S. Mark at Venice (PLATE XII, opposite). The original church, which stood where S. Mark's now stands, was destroyed by fire. In 977 the new building was begun, and was probably carried out mainly by builders from Byzantium, for, with the exception of minor details of later date, it is purely Byzantine in character. Those who have not visited Venice will be familiar, from photographs and drawings, with the form of S. Mark's richly incrusted front, a façade worthy of the picture which Ruskin draws in his "Stones of Venice": "a multitude of pillars and white domes, clustered into a long low pyramid of coloured light; a treasure-heap, it seems, partly of gold, and partly of opal and mother-of-pearl, hollowed beneath into five great vaulted porches, ceiled with fair mosaic, and beset with sculpture of alabaster, clear as amber and delicate as ivory. And round the walls of the porches there are set pillars of variegated stones, jasper and porphyry, and deep-green serpentine spotted with flakes of snow, and marbles, that half refuse and half yield to the sunshine,

PLATE XII — S. Mark's, Venice

Cleopatra-like, 'their bluest veins to kiss,'—the shadow, as it steals back from them, revealing line after line of azure undulation, as a receding tide leaves the waved sand; their capitals rich with interwoven tracery, rooted knots of herbage, and drifting leaves of acanthus and vine, and mystical signs, all beginning and ending in the Cross; and above them, in the broad archivolts, a continuous chain of language and of life—angels, and the signs of heaven, and the labours of men, each in its appointed season upon the earth; and above these, another range of glittering pinnacles, mixed with white arches, edged with scarlet flowers—a confusion of delight, amidst which the breasts of the Greek horses are seen blazing in their breadth of golden strength."

Though not so imposing a building as S. Sophia, S. Mark's is far superior to it as a manifestation of mosaic. The mosaics of S. Mark's do not "adorn" the church, they compose it—they are used, not decoratively, but structurally throughout. All the upper part is composed of curves, no sharp edges nor a correct right angle. "Vaults melt into one another; nowhere is the material broken. We receive an impression of an interior substantially composed of gold." [3]

Colour, which is the essence of life with orientals, does not enter greatly into the life or architecture of the West. The Byzantine style has had little influence upon the architecture of Western Europe. In Greece and Russia it became, and has continued to be, the recognised style for buildings of the Greek Church, though it has naturally received many modifications.

[3] L. March Philipps, "Form and Colour."

When Constantinople fell into the hands of the Turks (1453), the old architecture was revived, and was applied to the building of mosques, so that it was destined to exert considerable influence upon the building forms of the Moslems.

CHAPTER V
SARACENIC ARCHITECTURE

WE have seen that Christianity in its early days had little influence upon architecture, and that it did little towards asserting itself in this direction during the first 300 years of its existence. Far different was it with respect to a new religious movement which sprang up while the Byzantine empire was at the height of its power, in the sixth century of the Christian era—a movement which rapidly infected the East, sweeping over whole countries with an irresistible tide, and at once leaving its impress upon every phase of art.

Mohammed, the leader of the new faith, lived from A.D. 570–652. So sudden was the growth of his influence that within a century after his death he was acknowledged as the Prophet of God in Arabia, Egypt and Syria, in Persia, in India as far as the Ganges, along the north of Africa, and in Spain. Under these circumstances the Mohammedan, or, as it is more generally called, the Saracenic, a new architectural style, grew up, differing widely from the contemporary Christian architecture, and differing also in each of the various countries in which it prevailed.

The Arabs, who were the banner-bearers of the new Prophet, were a nomad and warlike race, but they were not great builders; they possessed, in fact, but little architecture of their own before the period of their conquests. As might be expected then, the earliest Mohammedan places of worship, or mosques, as they are called, were insignificant, and of simple form. Even at Mecca, the birthplace of the Prophet, the only temple of the Arabs—the sacred Kaabah—was nothing more than a square tower of little architectural importance.

The Koran, the sacred book of religious duties and precepts, contained no instructions for the followers of Mohammed with regard to the building of places of assembly or of worship. The faithful had their stated times for prayer when, turning their faces towards Mecca, they went through the prescribed forms; but for these ceremonies it was not necessary that there should be any assembling together: each man could offer up his prayers upon his own housetop. Nor were the mosques required—as in the case of temples of other religions—for the purpose of enshrining a sacred object or an image of the Deity, for Mecca was the one place sacred to all Mohammedans.

At first, then, there was little building in connection with the new religion: such mosques as were erected were merely shelters for purposes of prayer and retirement, of simplest form and, in the majority of cases, adapted from old buildings. When the Arabs began to erect new mosques, being without an architecture of their own, they were obliged to employ the native architects and workmen—a fact which accounts for the considerable differences of styles found in the different countries.

The most important of the early works were the mosques of Amrow at Cairo (A.D. 642), and of El Aksah (A.D. 690) at Jerusalem. These earlier buildings generally took the form of arcaded cloisters with flat timber roofs one storey high, enclosing a large square courtyard. On the side towards Mecca the cloister was much deeper and contained several rows of columns. On this plan was the magnificent mosque of Ibn Touloun, also at Cairo, built towards the end of the ninth century. Here the arcades of pointed arches spring from series of columns. On the side of the building nearest Mecca the arcades are five deep; in the centre of the outer wall on this side is the *mihrab*, or prayer-niche, indicating the direction of the sacred city, one of the indispensable features of the mosque-plan. At an early date minarets were added—slender towers from which the call to prayer was made to the Mohammedans throughout the city. The minarets assumed varied elegant forms, and added much picturesqueness to the exterior design. Usually they were octagonal, upon a square base, the upper part being circular, and marked by a projecting balcony from which the prayer-call was sounded. The roofs of the earlier mosques were flat and of wooden construction, but towards the end of the tenth century vaulting was introduced; and the vaulted roofs soon became one of the most characteristic, as they were the most beautiful, of the features of Saracenic architecture. In the tombs of the Caliphs, built in the eleventh century, and in the mosques of Barkouk (1149), of Sultan Hassan (1356), and of Kait Bey (1470), all at Cairo (PLATE XIV, p. 114, and PLATE XV, p. 116), we find not only this form of roof, but increasing skill in workmanship and richness of design. The mosque of Sultan Hassan, of which the interior court is shown in the illustration, is one of the finest examples of Saracenic art. Equally pleasing and more graceful externally, is that of Kait Bey with its characteristic minaret, dome and loggia.

Every example shows that the architecture of the Arabs was essentially decorative rather than structural; it was all typical of Arab character—fantastic and capricious. Generally the domes were decorated with rich and intricate geometric designs; similar or more elaborate treatment was applied to the whole of the interior. The dome—after the Byzantine fashion—

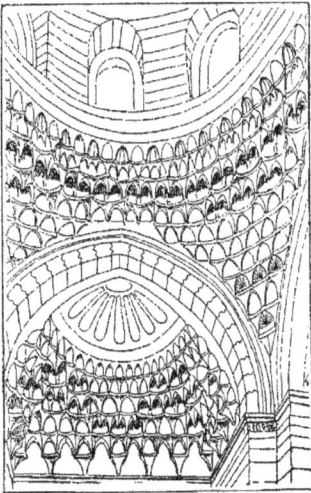

FIGURE 40 — *Honeycomb Corbelling to Pendentives, Mosque of Sultan Hassan*

was carried on pendentives, which were richly decorated with honeycomb ornament. This honeycomb corbelling was constantly used by the Arabs in their roofs, for it proved an effective method of filling up the awkward corners resulting from the practice of carrying octagonal walls upon a square base. The whole of the mosque interior was treated with lavish decoration, in which colour played a most important part.

PLATE XIV — *Mosque of Kait Bey, Cairo*

Ceilings were panelled out with intricately carved beams and were enriched with harmonious patterns; niches were resplendent with brightly coloured honeycomb roof-corbels; all the wall surfaces were incrusted with exquisite marbles or with brilliant arrangements of tiles, in which the Arab showed his fertility of invention equally with his feeling for colour. In accordance with the rules laid down in the Koran, no imitation of natural objects was permitted in the decoration; the designers were therefore restricted to the use of flowing and geometric patterns, which thus became characteristic of their work. In many cases inscriptions from the Koran were introduced, the ornamental Arabic lettering forming a very effective embellishment. An interesting feature, which marks the architecture of the Arabs to the present day, was the delicate tracery which frequently filled the windows and the wall-openings with complicated geometric designs.

In addition to the semi-circular arch, three other forms are found in Mohammedan buildings for the arcades and door-openings. In Syria and Egypt occurs the pointed arch, similar to that used by the Gothic architects of Western Europe. In India and in Persia the most common form has the curves near the apex bent slightly upwards, giving to the arch an outline like the keel of a vessel; this form is sometimes called the keel arch. The third form, the horse-shoe arch, is most frequently met with amongst the works of the Moors in Spain.

Mention of the Moors recalls the fact that some of the most splendid examples of Arabic architecture are

PLATE XV — *Mosque of Sultan Hassan, Cairo*

found farther west and in our own Continent. With the exception of the mosques of Cairo, few important works were produced in Northern Africa. When, however, the Moors invaded Spain, in 710, there sprang up in that country a new Arabian empire, whose architecture was destined to rival that of the East.

The first important building was the mosque at Cordova, begun in 786 by the Caliph Abder-Rahman. This consisted of an arcaded hall in the form of a parallelogram 420 feet by 375 feet—thus covering a larger area than any Christian church, with the exception of S. Peter's in Rome. The height however, was not more than 30 feet; the ceiling was of wood richly carved and decorated, and was carried upon seventeen rows of thirty-three columns each, all having two tiers of horse-shoe arches. The mihrab-niche, indicating the direction of Mecca, was richly incrusted with delicate carving and with mosaics. This sanctuary at Cordova, which was rebuilt in the tenth century, is considered by Fergusson to be "the most beautiful and elaborate specimen of Moorish architecture in Spain, and of the best age." Unfortunately but little of the great mosque remains in its original state.

Fate has been kinder to the great citadel palace at Granada, known as the Alhambra—the Mecca of travellers in Spain at the present day. This great work was begun in 1248 by Mohammed-ben-Alhamar, after his expulsion from Seville, and was completed in the beginning of the fourteenth century. Those who have not been able to visit the Alhambra are afforded the

From an Engraving by Owen Jones.

FIGURE 41 — *Entrance to the Court of the Lions, Alhambra*

opportunity of studying the wealth of its design in the magnificent illustrations and drawings of Owen Jones.

The Alhambra is considered the gem of Hispano-Moresque art—a distinction due as much to its excellent state of preservation as to the delicate beauty of its work. Two large courts occupy the greater portion of the ground plan: the more celebrated of these, the Court of the Lions, is surrounded by light arcades, with a central fountain supported by twelve lions, from which it takes its name. The whole of the interior is covered with delicate ornamentation of exquisite beauty, to which the harmonious colouring adds wonderful richness and charm.

The Alcazar (castle) at Seville, an earlier building than the Alhambra, was probably even more magnificent, but it has become much dilapidated, and its character has been destroyed by alterations. Of greater interest, in the present day, is the Giralda in the same city, a building in the form of a massive square tower, not unlike a minaret on a grand scale. Unlike the Moslem builders in the East, however, the Moors in Spain never built minarets in connection with their mosque architecture, and the Giralda appears not to have been constructed for the purpose of the call to prayer.

Saracenic architecture flourished in Spain until the reconquest of the country by the Christians and the expulsion of the Moors in 1492. The Moors had obtained a footing also in Sicily, whence they were driven out at the end of the eleventh century, leaving behind them buildings which very strongly influenced the architecture of the Christian builders who succeeded them in the island.

Upon the capture of Constantinople by the Turks in 1453, the Christian churches there fell into the hands of the Mohammedans. The church of Hagia Sophia, the masterpiece of the Byzantine builders, was at once converted into a mosque, and, strange to say, served as the model for the architecture which sprang up to meet the new religious requirements. The new style culminated, just a century later, in the Suleimaniyeh, the great mosque built by Soliman the Magnificent in 1553.

CHAPTER VI

ROMANESQUE ARCHITECTURE

We must now hark back to Italy, where the early Christians were left at work upon their basilicas.

The transference of the seat of government by Constantine to Byzantium, and the consequent decay of the Roman empire, checked intelligent building for a period in Italy. But, as Christianity continued to spread, there was an increasing demand for accommodation on the part of its adherents, and builders were called upon to provide it, first in this town, then in the other. Throughout the Dark Ages—from the fifth to the tenth century—a considerable amount of building was done, but very little architecture was produced worthy of the name, except in those cities in which, as at Ravenna and Venice, it was developed under Byzantine auspices. Meanwhile, however, the Church was strengthening her authority and broadening her influences, and a new style of architecture slowly developed—with natural modifications arising out of climatic and other local conditions—and gradually spread throughout Western Europe. This new architecture, based upon the traditions of Rome and of the early Christian builders of that city, received the name of *Romanesque.*

Although Rome's influence was impressed upon the Byzantine style of architecture as well as upon that which we here call Romanesque, it is desirable to keep one style quite distinct from the other. The two showed marked differences from the beginning; and when the Churches of Rome and of Byzantium diverged upon questions affecting the ritual and the creed, the divergence became still greater in the architecture of the Eastern and the Western Churches. That of the Eastern Church—the Orthodox Church, so-called— had never departed from the Byzantine models, and the influence of Byzantium has thus spread throughout Greece, Asia Minor and Russia. On the other hand, the Western Church has always looked to Rome for her earliest inspirations and has drawn upon the mother- city for her architecture, though different countries have, naturally, developed their own characteristic features.

To deal first with Italy. During the formative period, which may be said to have ended with the tenth century, architecture—such as it was—was almost entirely ecclesiastical. The basilican churches were the natural outcome of the situation in Rome, where basilicas were to hand to serve as models, and where on all sides classic temples, with their choice columns and marble wall- linings, were available for the Christian despoiler. But away from Rome other conditions prevailed; materials were necessarily simpler, and greater originality was required on the part of the architects, in order to invest their designs with dignity and interest. Bitter experience also had taught the need of replacing the low wooden roofs of the basilica by a more enduring form of vaulted construction.

In due course, then, it came about that in Italy three distinct styles of Romanesque architecture were developed: the Basilican, or Early Christian—which, as we have seen, continued to prevail in Rome—the Lombard, and the Tuscan, or Pisan.

The Lombard style, as the name denotes, flourished chiefly in the cities of the Lombardy Plain, in the north of Italy, from Milan on the west to Bologna on the east. These two cities, and their neighbours, Piacenza, Verona and Pavia, all contain good examples of the style in S. Zeno (Verona), S. Ambrogio (Milan), the cathedral of Piacenza, and others.

The old church of S. Zeno at Verona, of the twelfth century, shows many characteristic features. The façade was simple in composition, with a fine breadth of flat surface, emphasised at intervals by a series of arcades filled in with slender columns and arches, or by arcaded corbels carved under the slopes of the gable. Long, slender pilasters divided the front into three parts, thus suggesting the interior nave-and-aisle division of the basilica; some of the early basilican features were lost externally, and the low-pitched roof was concealed behind a simple gable. A rose-window occupied the space under the centre of the gable, and beneath this a projecting porch marked the doorway. The columns of the portico rested upon the backs of crouching

FIGURE 42 — *S. Zeno, Verona*

lions—familiar features to all who have visited the old cities of Lombardy. Elaborate, grotesque carving enriched the entrance, and atoned somewhat for the severe treatment of the upper portion of the front. The façades were always solemn and dignified, and, with their slender columns and lightly projecting arcades, relied upon the crisp Italian sunlight for relief and for vigorous effects of light and shade; else they were inclined to gloominess and severity. Tennyson, visiting these cities under a dull sky, noted how—

Stem and sad (so rare the smiles
Of sunlight) look'd the Lombard piles;
Porch-pillars on the lion resting,
And sombre, old, colonnaded aisles.

In connection with many of the churches, as at S. Zeno, Verona, and the cathedral at Piacenza, was found a square campanile or bell-tower, simple in form and always well-proportioned.

Internally the plan of the Lombard churches resembled the old basilicas, with such modifications as were required by the introduction of the massive vaulted roofs—*e.g.,* the reduction in width of the nave and the substitution of sturdy piers for the rows of graceful columns. Sometimes a crypt and shrine were found beneath the choir, the floor of the choir being raised a few steps above the general floor level.

The Tuscan-Romanesque was not unlike the Lombard, modified by the different social conditions which existed in Florence, Pisa and the neighbouring cities of Tuscany. The finest examples are found at Pisa, where the Romanesque buildings in the Piazza—the cathedral (A.D. 1063–1100), the baptistery (A.D. 1153), and the leaning tower (A.D. 1174)—form one of the most interesting architectural groups in Italy (PLATE XIII, p. 127).

The Tuscan designs are lighter and more elegant than those of the northern cities. Timber ceilings were adhered to, in connection with the basilican forms, permitting the use of columns instead of piers for the interior nave-and-aisle divisions. The façades were

almost entirely covered with a lavish arrangement
of wall-arcades and galleries, as seen in the Pisan
buildings; or they were divided into panels of dark
and white marbles, as at S. Miniato in Florence. The
arcading was highly decorative, the tendency to become
monotonous being in most instances averted by skilful
and varied treatment of the different tiers. The tower at
Pisa forms an exception, for the constant repetition of
bands of arcades of almost equal height, from the base
to the summit, destroys the interest of the building as
an architectural design, and almost justifies Ruskin's
description of it as "the one thoroughly ugly tower in
Italy."

Tuscan-Romanesque was much influenced by the
Byzantine methods of building and of decoration, for
Pisa was a port maintaining an extensive trade with
Byzantium. This fact probably accounts for the use of
the marble panelling, which became characteristic of
Florentine architecture, and influenced that of the later
Gothic period.

Lucca and Pistoja, neighbours of Florence, have
good examples of the Pisan style; and in many parts of
Italy churches were erected to which the generic term
Romanesque may be applied, in which were blended the
methods and traditions of the Byzantine, the Lombard,
and the Tuscan builders.

In Sicily, the rule of the Mohammedans, which
began A.D. 827, and lasted through two centuries, left its
impress upon the island's architecture, so that we find
Arabic influences mingled with those of Byzantium,

PLATE XIII — *Piazza del Duomo, Pisa*

Greece and Italy. The beautiful cathedral of Monreale, near Palermo (A.D. 1175), is built upon a basilican plan, and reveals a picturesque mixture of the different styles. The nave columns have finely carved capitals

Drawn by W. Eden Nesfield.

FIGURE 43 — *East End, Lucca Cathedral*

of the distinctive Byzantine form with the *dosseret* supporting pointed arches. A dado of white marble lines the lower portion of the walls, above which they are richly incrusted with mosaics representing Biblical stories. The timber roof is somewhat elaborate, and is richly treated with colour decoration, after the manner of the Mohammedan interiors.

During the first ten centuries of the Christian era architecture made little progress in Europe, outside of Italy and of the eastern countries which came more directly under Roman influence. Spain alone, in the West, had become a flourishing centre of the art, thanks to the incursion of the Moors. Throughout this period society in Western Europe was in a state of chaos; lawlessness was rife, and progress in architecture or in any of the fine arts was impossible. The church alone, as an institution, showed some little vitality, for within its monastic walls prevailed a peace which was unaffected by the external turmoil and unrest. Building on an extensive scale was, moreover, checked by a very widespread belief in the theory of the impending end of the world in the year 1000; but this check was a temporary one, for the fear of the dread event led many an uneasy conscience to contribute liberally to the monasteries, or to seek refuge in them; the new century, therefore, found these institutions wealthy and powerful as they had never been before. A period of great activity ensued, and architecture at once began to make considerable progress in all directions.

Almost all the new buildings of importance were ecclesiastical, and the builders naturally looked to Rome as their centre and their source of technical help and inspiration. But, to many, Rome was a far-off country, and the new occasions taught new methods and devices which soon made the term Romanesque a very comprehensive title, for under this head may be conveniently classed all the "round-arched Gothic" which prevailed throughout the west of Europe before the introduction of the true Gothic, and which in England culminated in the "Norman" buildings of the eleventh and twelfth centuries.

The architecture of each country, governed by local conditions and traditions, was marked by its own distinctive features, but showed at the same time a general similarity of style. Almost all the buildings were constructed with the same object, and it became a question of solving the same problem in different ways— the problem, namely, of combining the vaulted roof construction with the basilican plan. The heavy "barrel-vault" of the roof demanded massive walls and piers, and the use of the semicircular arch required piers or very sturdy columns at frequent intervals. The resulting style was of necessity somewhat ponderous, so that relief was sought in rich carving and in a multiplicity of recessed spaces; and the architects did not successfully grapple with the difficulty until the introduction—in the twelfth and thirteenth centuries—of *ribbed* vaulting, which, with the pointed Gothic arch, revolutionised the conditions of construction, and gave the builders a happy and complete solution of their problem. What is called "Gothic" architecture is in reality nothing more than the logical outcome of the progressive Romanesque; the transition is a natural one, just as, in English architecture, is the transition from the round-arched Norman to the pointed style of the thirteenth century. The name "Gothic" is an unfortunate one, for readers are apt to regard it as a foreign and distinct style, breaking in upon, and interrupting the continuity of, the architecture of the period. It is only by following the Romanesque architects in their constructive difficulties with the round arch that we are able to appreciate what the Gothic principles did for their architecture, and the extent to which they enlarged its scope.

To turn now to France. In the Romanesque buildings of this country may be traced the results of various influences. Many of the southern churches possessed marked Byzantine features, the outcome of a very considerable trade which was carried on between the ports on the south coast, Venice, and the east. In the church of S. Front at Périgueux (A.D. 1047), the plan strikingly resembles that of S. Mark's, Venice; the interior is roofed over with domes in a similar manner, but they are constructed externally in stone, instead of having false wooden roofs as the domes of S. Mark's. The interior of the building is finished in stone, with none of the rich interior decoration of the Venetian church. At Cahors is a domed cathedral of the same date, undoubtedly copied from a church in Byzantium. In other parts of the country the designs were influenced by the examples of classic Roman buildings, such as those found at Nîmes, Arles, Avignon, etc. In the churches

FIGURE 44 — *Capital in the Abbey Church, Fécamp*

of Notre Dame at Avignon, and S. Trophîme at Arles, we find Corinthian capitals, pilasters, enrichments, and other features borrowed directly from the classic models.

Auvergne contains some excellent examples of Romanesque churches, built of the lava of this well-known volcanic district. Let us consider the church of Notre Dame du Port at Clermont-Ferrand, an excellent

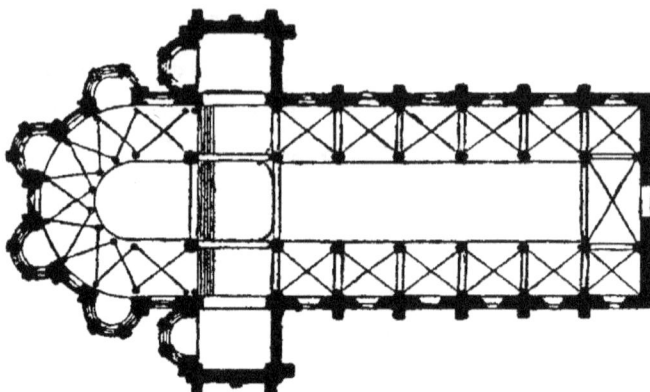

FIGURE 45 — *Plan of Notre Dame du Port, Clermont-Ferrand*

and typical example of the style. Lava is used in the construction, and some effect is gained by the use of lavas of different colours. The plan of this church shows a long nave covered by barrel vaulting, with small transepts and an apsidal end. Round the apse is carried a series of small apsidal chapels. These small apses, built round the main apse, form what is called a *chevet,* which became an essential feature in French cathedral plans. Such a group of small chapels, ranged round the end of a lofty cathedral, produces a singularly interesting and dignified interior effect. The feature was introduced by the Romanesque builders, and probably originated in the Auvergne district, where it is found in the Romanesque churches at Issoire, Le Puy, Clermont-Ferrand and elsewhere. The Gothic architects retained the *chevet,* so that it figures in the plans of most of the great French cathedrals of that period.

The chief constructional difficulty with which the Romanesque builders had to contend was the method of support for the massive barrel-vaulted roofs which covered the naves. The old Romans, as we saw, escaped the trouble of side-thrusts and strains by building up their vaulted roofs and domes in solid concrete, so that the mass rested securely upon the walls without any lateral thrust, just as a lid rests upon a box. But stone vaulting exerted a *lateral* thrust, which required to be counteracted by means of heavy abutments, or buttresses. The illustration shows an outline section of

FIGURE 46 — *Section through Notre Dame du Port, Clermont-Ferrand*

Notre Dame du Port, which indicates the method of buttressing adopted. Here the thrust of the great barrel vault over the nave would tend to push apart the walls upon which it rests. This thrust is counteracted by the use of half-barrel vaults over the aisles. A glance at the section will show that such an arrangement made it impossible to light the upper part by means of clerestory windows; the nave vault was therefore dependent upon brilliant weather to relieve it from a state of gloom.

In some examples, as at Autun (A.D. 1150), clerestory windows were introduced, the nave vault being raised sufficiently high for the purpose above the roofs of the side aisles; but the constructive methods were not equal to the task, for in almost all cases the vaults gave way and required to be reconstructed. Towards the end of the twelfth century the use of flying buttresses to resist the lateral thrusts made it possible to combine clerestory windows with barrel vaults; but the difficulty was not satisfactorily surmounted until the introduction of groined vaults in the thirteenth century.

We cannot take leave of the Romanesque buildings of France without touching upon the works of the great Norman Dukes—so intimately connected with the architecture of our own island.

The best known example among the abbey churches of Normandy, and one of the noblest buildings of the time, was the Abbaye-aux-Hommes, or S. Etienne, at Caen (PLATE XVI, opposite), begun in 1066 by William of Normandy—better known to us as William the Conqueror—in commemoration of his victory at Hastings. The church is lofty in its proportions, with nave, aisles and transept. Its east end was originally in the form of a simple apse, but this has been superseded by the *chevet*; the west front is finely proportioned and is flanked by two towers, between which the nave rests. The spires which crown the towers are later additions. The nave and aisles are vaulted, and a clerestory is obtained by a series of flying buttresses. The system of vaulting is of interest as illustrating the stage which preceded the introduction of the pointed arch, and

PLATE XVI — *Exterior, Abbaye-aux-Hommes, Caen*

PLATE XVII — *Abbaye-aux-Dames, Caen*

the consequent solution of the constructive difficulties which were constantly baffling the builders of this period.

Of equal interest is William of Normandy's other great building, the Abbaye-aux-Dames, or S. Trinité, at Caen (1083), (PLATE XVII, opposite). The fine church of Mont S. Michel has undergone many alterations in later times, and, like many cathedral and other churches in Normandy and Brittany (and in England), has lost much of its original character.

GERMANY.—Romanesque architecture in Germany followed somewhat closely on the lines of that of North Italy, as might be expected, for there was constant communication between the two countries, and a large German population in Milan. Indeed, the Lombard-Romanesque of North Italy may be said to have emanated from Germany.

Of the earlier buildings the cathedral at Aix-la-Chapelle, built by Charlemagne (about 800) is interesting, architecturally as an imitation of S. Vitale at Ravenna, and historically as the crowning place of the Western emperors. It is a polygonal building of sixteen sides, surmounted by an octagonal dome.

Before the thirteenth century the art of building did not make great progress in any parts of Germany other than Saxony and the Rhenish provinces; in the districts of the Rhine, however, Romanesque architecture may be said to have developed more fully than in any other country in Europe. The exterior of the Rhenish churches was characterised by picturesque grouping of

FIGURE 47 — *Church of the Apostles, Cologne*

octagonal turrets, the introduction of arcaded recesses
to decorate the lower portions of the wall-space, and
of open arcaded galleries under the gable-ends and
the cornices of the apses and turrets. The Church of
the Apostles at Cologne (1160–1200) is a successful
example of this treatment. The view in the illustration
shows the arrangement of the eastern portion, with
three apses opening off the central space of the choir—
an arrangement productive of dignified and noble
effect both externally and internally. The plan of the
building shows a tri-apsidal end and a broad nave,
flanked on either side by aisles of half its width. The
transepts are at the west end, and the crossing is covered
with a Byzantine dome carried on pendentives; the

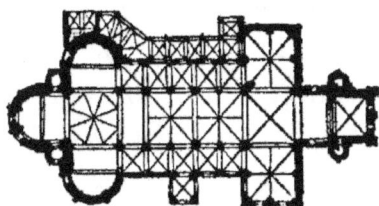

FIGURE 48 — *Plan of Church of the Apostles, Cologne*

nave has been vaulted at a later period. S. Maria im Kapitol (rebuilt 1047), and S. Martin (1150), both in Cologne, show similar characteristics, and make, with the Church of the Apostles, one of the most interesting groups of churches which the Romanesque period produced. The remarkable church of S. Gereon, also at Cologne, has a Romanesque nave and sacristy (1075). Other good German examples are the cathedrals of Mayence and Spires (both of the eleventh century), and Worms, all of which have vaulted naves of the twelfth century.

FIGURE 49 — *Worms Cathedral*

SPAIN.—Comparatively little Romanesque work is to be found in Spain, for throughout this period a great part of the country was under the dominion of the Moors. The capture of Toledo in 1062 paved the way for a series of successes of the Christians; but it was not until 1492 that the Moorish rule was entirely destroyed by the fall of Granada. Such churches as were built appear to have been constructed on the lines of the French churches of Auvergne.

The church of San Iago de Compostella (1080) is a good example, with nave and transepts, choir and *chevet*. In most instances, however, a departure was made from French tradition by the erection of a dome on pendentives over the crossing of the nave and transepts, as in the old cathedral at Salamanca (twelfth century). It is strange that no details of the Romanesque churches of Spain show traces of influence of the Moorish architecture which abounded on every side, though this may be accounted for by the fact that the Christians heartily hated the Mohammedans and everything that belonged to them.

GREAT BRITAIN.—The inhabitants of Great Britain appear to have troubled themselves little about architecture before the Norman conquest. Prior to this the most important building work was done by the Benedictines, to which Order belonged all the older monasteries in England—among others, the Benedictine Monastery which preceded Westminster Abbey, founded by S. Dunstan (A.D. 960). At Canterbury the recent excavations which have laid bare the floor and western front of S. Augustine's original Abbey Church reveal to us what is probably the earliest plan of a Benedictine church in Europe. Numerous churches were erected by the Saxons and the Celts, but the remains are sufficient only to prove that these early builders—of the "primitive Romanesque" period—were endowed with little technical skill. The tower of Earl's Barton, in Northants, and the little church at Bradford-on-Avon are perhaps the best existing examples of the work of the Saxons. The rare occurrence of Saxon remains at the present time is probably due to the fact that, with the advent of the Normans, the ruder primitive buildings

FIGURE 50 — *Tower, Earl's Barton, Northants*

were destroyed to make way for the new style which swept so rapidly over the country. Possibly, too, the generous use of wood in the construction led to decay. Timber was much in vogue among the earlier Saxons, and its use appears to have influenced the details of their later stone work. Their triangular headed window openings and "turned baluster" window mullions are certainly suggestive of timber construction.

Before the landing of William the Norman the influence of the Normans was beginning to make itself felt, for—England's insular position notwithstanding—it

FIGURE 51 — *Saxon Window, Earl's Barton*

was impossible that the country should be unaffected by the art which was making such gigantic strides within a few miles of its seaboard. The Norman conquest (1066), and the subsequent occupation of the country by the barons and ecclesiastics of Normandy, effected a rapid social revolution, and speedily transformed the political organisations of the island. As an immediate result of the change there set in a period of extraordinary activity in the building of churches, abbeys and castles, by means of which the invaders were enabled to establish themselves more securely upon the lands plundered from the conquered Saxons. Many churches were founded by the Norman himself, while his followers vied one with another in their efforts to surpass all that had been seen on the other side of the Channel.

The Romanesque, or—to use a more familiar term—the Norman period, during which the architecture imported by the invaders prevailed in England, lasted for a little more than a century—*i.e.*, from the conquest until the accession of Richard I, in 1189. Between these dates building operations were carried on throughout

England with almost incredible activity. Not only in many of our great cathedrals do we find extensive remains of Norman work, but in a vast number of churches in every part of the country fragments and details are found, pointing to the fact that a complete Norman structure once occupied the site, from which almost every trace of the original work has disappeared. It has been computed that no less than 7,000 churches were built within a century after the conquest.

The Romanesque, or "Norman," cathedral of England is marked by features similar to those which characterise the Romanesque buildings of Normandy. Its general appearance is sturdy, with solid walls, cushion-shaped capitals,

> Massive arches, broad and round
> On ponderous columns, short and low.

Compared with its Continental prototype, the typical Norman cathedral, such as that of Durham or Peterborough, is longer in proportion to its width, the length being especially marked in the choir. A square east end takes the place of the apse or *chevet* of French cathedrals, and the transepts are more important. A great central tower, carried over the crossing of the nave and transepts, is also characteristic of the English plan.

Internally there was generally the intention—suggested by the massive piers and columns—to vault over the aisles and the nave. The vaulted roofs, however, through lack of funds or other considerations, were seldom completed. Flat, low-pitched roofs and wooden ceilings were substituted; and as these were light and

Drawn by W. Samuel Weatheney.

FIGURE 52 — *Part of Nave, Durham Cathedral*

easily supported, the builders were able to insert large clerestory windows, and to secure light and lofty effect at little cost. The wooden roofs, however, were liable to injury from fire, and, in many instances, were burned or destroyed, so that in several cathedrals, as at Gloucester, Durham and Exeter, they were replaced at a later date by stone vaulting.

The details of our Norman churches, with few exceptions, are extremely simple; they are seen in

Figure 53 — *St. Mary's Chapel, Stourbridge*

their simplest form in the little chapel of S. Mary, at Stourbridge, near Cambridge. The piers were often perfectly plain and round, as at Gloucester; sometimes clustered, as at Peterborough; or, as at Durham, clustered and round piers were used alternately. Doorways were simple in outline, circular-headed, and with little of the added ornamentation which appeared in the gables of the later Gothic entrances; richly carved capitals decorated the clustered columns of the opening, and a profusion of carving covered the arch-mouldings. The design showed little variety; the zig-zag ornamentation, easily shaped with the axe, occurred with endless repetition, varied occasionally by the well-known "bird's-beak" moulding, familiar to the most casual observer of Norman work. Window openings were treated more simply than doorways, but were sometimes enriched with the zig-zag, as at Iffley Church, near Oxford, and occasionally with interlacing arches, as at Castle Rising Church. The cushion-shaped capitals, suggestive of the sturdy echinus of the Greek Doric column, were usually left quite plain, though the Norman mason took pleasure in carving quaint devices or grotesque faces upon the caps, or upon the projecting stones of the external corbel courses after the buildings had been completed.

FIGURE 54 — *Castle Rising Church,*
West Front before restoration

Portions of many of the old Norman structures have been rebuilt at a later date. The following list includes the principal monuments of the period in England. Less important, though not less interesting, are the examples found among the parish churches throughout the country:—

Canterbury Cathedral...... Crypt.

Carlisle Cathedral.......... Nave.

Ely Cathedral.............. Nave and Transepts.

Winchester Cathedral....... Transepts.

Waltham Abbey............ Choir.

Durham Cathedral......... Galilee Porch, Nave, and Chapter-house.

Peterborough Cathedral.... Nave.

Rochester Cathedral........ Nave.

Norwich Cathedral......... Nave.

Hereford Cathedral........ Nave and Choir.

Christ Church, Oxford...... Nave and Transepts.

Gloucester............... Nave.

Tower of London.......... White Chapel.

S. Alban's Abbey............ Nave, etc.

Church of S. Bartholomew the Great, London.

CHAPTER VII

GOTHIC ARCHITECTURE

THE Romanesque architects on the Continent, as we have seen, had made great progress in the art of building by the middle of the twelfth century, and had mastered most of the problems which had puzzled their predecessors, so that their architecture throughout Europe—especially in the north and west—had regained much of its lost dignity. But they had not yet arrived at a successful method of roof treatment. The wooden roof was unsatisfactory, and led to destruction by fire of many a substantial building; while the alternative to this, the barrel-vaulting, which had been used in the buildings of the old Romans, was too ponderous. True, the "lids" of solid concrete with which the Romans covered their vast buildings exerted no *lateral* pressure upon the walls, but their enormous weight required equally massive walls to carry them. When masonry took the place of concrete, the vaults were still more difficult to support, for the arched form of the heavy vault tended to force the walls apart—exerted a lateral thrust, as we say—so that it was necessary, not only to make the walls massive and strong, but also to reduce the span, or width of the vaulted spaces.

The Romanesque builders worked out a system of construction with preliminary arches or ribs, and it was in the efforts of the later architects to find a solution to the roof difficulties, and in their gradual recognition of the aesthetic possibilities of the rib, that they developed the great principle of *ribbed vaulting*—a principle which brought about nothing less than a revolution in the art of building, and which, in fact, formed the structural basis of the style of architecture known as "Gothic."

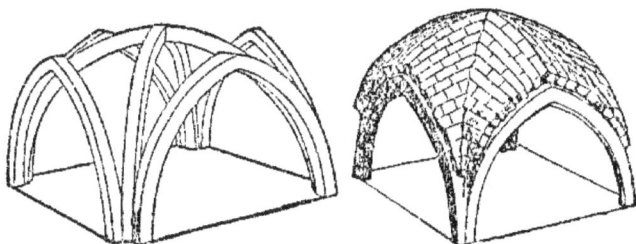

FIGURE 55 — *Gothic Ribbed Vaulting*

This new principle at once infused into architecture the new quality of *energy*, as distinguished from that strength in repose, which characterised the Romanesque.

The term Gothic is as unfortunate as it is inapt. Gothic architecture is the natural outcome of Romanesque, though the term seems to suggest a break in the progressive character of the art, and has doubtless proved a stumbling block to many students, by leading them to regard the styles as distinct from, and possibly opposed to, one another. "Gothic" was merely a contemptuous term applied to the style by the classical enthusiasts of the Renaissance, who looked upon a Goth as a typical barbarian, and who regarded anything nonclassical as barbarous; but the name has stuck, as bad names have a habit of doing, and is still in general use to denote the pointed style which developed in the twelfth, and flourished in the succeeding centuries. The pointed arch, it should be noted, was in reality incidental to the development of Gothic, though it is usual to consider it the characteristic feature of the style.

In ribbed vaulting, a skeleton vault is formed of ribs carried transversely and diagonally across the nave, so as to form a strong open framework, and to concentrate the weight and pressure of the roof upon the isolated points of support from which the ribs spring, the spaces between the ribs being then filled in with lighter masonry. The advantages of this form of construction are readily seen; the roof became lighter, and could span larger areas; and, as the pressure was concentrated upon certain points, it was necessary only to strengthen the wall at these points, instead of making it thick and massive throughout. Buttresses were introduced for this purpose; and as the wall between the buttresses, relieved from the pressure of the roof, became now of secondary importance—for it was merely a screen to keep out the weather—it could be constructed of light materials, or opened up in the form of windows. With this innovation, then—the application of the principles of *concentration of strains* and of *balanced thrusts*— the Early Gothic builders took up the constructive problems just where the Romanesque builders were being baffled by them, and soon added fresh dignity and grandeur to their work.

Let us see to what extent these new principles affected design and construction. The illustration shows the plan of a highly developed Gothic building of simple form, Sainte Chapelle in Paris, built by Louis IX (1243–1247). The upper chapel here is an unbroken room, 100 feet in length, 33 feet wide, and 60 feet in height, roofed over with a series of groined vaults springing from slender columns. The thrust of

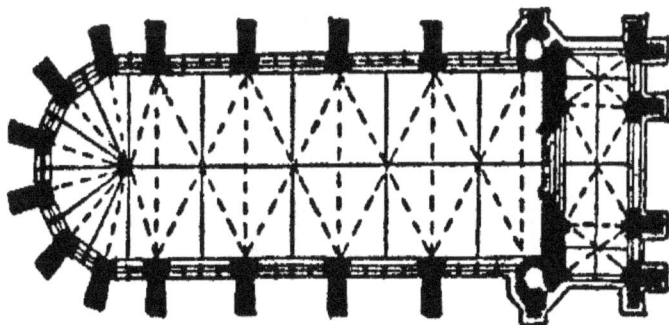

FIGURE 56 — *Plan of Sainte Chapelle*

the columns is taken by buttresses—very sturdy, as we see in the plan—and carried up the entire height of the exterior walls. Now note that the massive walls, which would have been necessary to support such a superstructure in Romanesque work, have disappeared. The wall lengths between each vault have, so to speak, been turned round upon their axes, and placed at right angles to their original direction, so as to form a series of buttresses, with abutment sufficient to withstand the thrust of the groined roof-vaulting. These wall spaces between the buttresses are no longer required for constructive purposes, and can therefore be filled with large windows, destined soon, as a natural further development, to become rich with the glories of stained glass.

In a design such as Sainte Chapelle, a Gothic church without aisles, the problem of dealing with the thrusts is presented in its simpler form, as the walls which take the thrusts are *external* walls. But when aisles are introduced at the side of the nave, a fresh difficulty arises. The buttresses cannot now be carried vertically down, for they would block up the aisles with their mass. To permit of their being ranged along the external face of the aisle-walls, a new feature is brought into play—the flying buttress, which bridges over the intervening space, and supplies at once the necessary counterthrust to the roof-vaulting of the nave. As the nave piers and the walls over them are now relieved, by the buttresses, of the more serious part of their burden, and have to perform only the simple task of carrying the vertical weight, the builders are enabled to make them not only lofty, but slighter and more graceful.

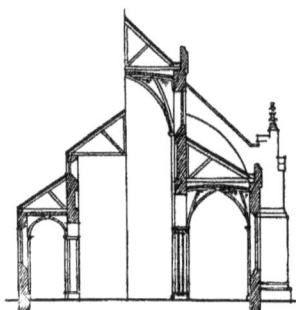

FIGURE 57 — *Romanesque Contrasted with Gothic*

The flying buttress, then, soon became a characteristic feature of Gothic building. True, its necessary presence hampered the exterior design in some respects, but its decorative possibilities were speedily recognised and seized upon. So ornate and ornamental did it become that in many French cathedrals it has the appearance of being a purely decorative feature, placed in its position for no other reason than to delight the eye and to endow the design with grace, and with that

FIGURE 58 — *Flying Buttress, Beauvais Cathedral*

suggestion of aspiration—rather than repose—which is inseparably connected with true Gothic:

> The Grecian gluts me with its perfectness,
> Unanswerable as Euclid—self-contained;
>
> . . . .
>
> But ah! this other, this that never ends,
> Still climbing, luring fancy still to climb,
> Imagination's very self in stone.

While the buttress enabled the builder to introduce height into his design as one of the chief elements of effect, the pointed arch solved the difficulty of bridging over varying widths at any required height. The Gothic architect could thus give play to his fancy and imagination, little troubled by problems of construction, and unfettered by considerations of precedent.

From a Drawing by F. Saunders.

FIGURE 59 — *Windows of late Gothic Period,*
S. Peter Mancroft, Norwich

The Gothic cathedral has been styled "a roof of stone with walls of glass," and not inaptly; for the walls, no longer required to be of massive construction to carry the weight, became little more than screens, either of masonry or of glass, filling in the spaces between the buttresses, to keep out the weather and to give effect to the design; and no treatment of these spaces could secure so glorious a result as did the introduction of great traceried windows filled with richly coloured glass.

So beautiful was the painted glass of the period that it at once made its influence felt upon the architecture; the windows were increased in size, and the walls, as far as possible, were illuminated. "Far more important," remarks Fergusson, "than the introduction of the pointed arch was the invention of painted glass, which is really the important formative principle of Gothic architecture; so much so, that there would be more meaning in the name if it were called the *'painted-glass style'* instead of the pointed-arch style. . . . We must bear in mind that all windows in all churches erected after the middle of the twelfth century were filled, or were intended to be filled, with painted glass, and that the principal and guiding motive in all the changes subsequently introduced into the architecture of the age was to obtain the greatest possible space and the best localities for its display."

The extensive use of glass soon led to a great development of another feature—window tracery. The nature of the glass required that the window areas which it filled should be divided up into a number of smaller spaces. Thus, although perhaps no feature of Gothic design appears more purely ornamental than the elaborate tracery of the windows, it has, like almost all decorative parts, a constructional *raison d' être*, forming, in fact, part of the skeleton of the Gothic frame. The attention given by designers to tracery led it, by gradual stages, from simple beginnings to a period of florid elaboration, so that by this feature, more readily than by any other, it is possible to trace the various periods in the history of Gothic architecture.

FRANCE.—Gothic architecture in France, the country of its birth, may be divided into three periods, of which the approximate dates are:

Early Period (*circa* 1160–1270).

Middle Period (*circa* 1270–1370).

Florid or Flamboyant Period (*circa* 1370–1550).

The second half of the twelfth century was a period of extraordinary activity with the French cathedral builders. The Church at this time was a strong and popular institution. Many of its cathedrals, built by the careful but unscientific Romanesque builders, were

FIGURE 60 — *Capital, S. Germain des Prés, Paris*

collapsing under the weights of their ponderous vaults, and were in urgent need of renovation. In other parts new structures were required, and with such energy did the bishops, backed up by the people, set to work that, at the end of the twelfth century, as many as sixteen cathedrals were being built, or entirely reconstructed, among them—to give only the more familiar names— being those of Bayonne, Lisieux, Laon, Tours, Poitiers, Troyes, Chartres, Bourges and Notre Dame, Paris.

The buildings of this date were marked by simplicity of treatment of the groined vaulting, of the arrangement of parts and of the detail; the carving was simple and vigorous, the windows long and narrow, and frequently grouped in pairs beneath a pointed arch, the head pierced with a circular light, as in our plate-tracery. The interior division into bays was marked on the exterior by a uniform series of pinnacled flying buttresses. A steep wooden roof, covered with lead or tiles, completed the structure, protecting and allowing space inside for the lofty stone vaulting. In some of the finest buildings of the period are found magnificent capitals with carving derived from the Corinthian acanthus foliage, as in the church of S. Germain des Prés, Paris.

Notre Dame, Paris (1163–1214), one of the earliest, shows a perfectly symmetrical plan with semi-circular east end, richly sculptured triple western portals, rose-windows in the chief gables, and most of the characteristic features of the French cathedral of the thirteenth century.

Later in date than Notre Dame was the graceful cathedral of Chartres (1194–1230), the richly decorated northern spire of which, added in the sixteenth century, contrasts in an instructive manner with the simple and beautiful lines of its southern companion. The magnificent windows—

> Pride of France,
> Each the bright gift of some mechanic guild,
> Who loved their city, and thought gold well spent
> To make her beautiful with piety—

THE STORY OF ARCHITECTURE

are filled with a glorious setting of stained glass, a lasting memorial of the interest and enthusiasm which all classes displayed in the building of their temple.

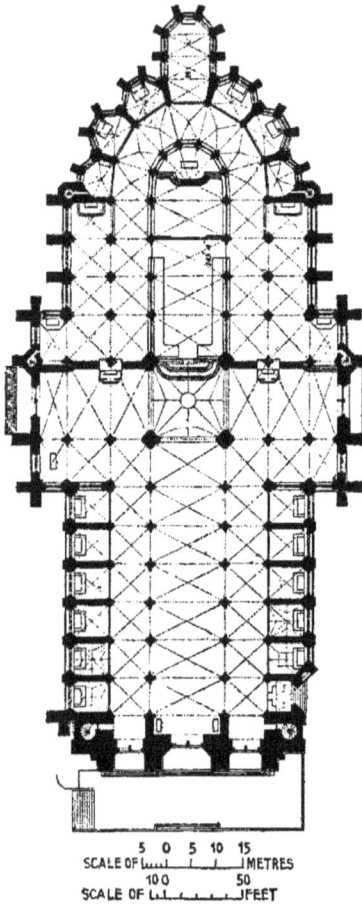

In the beautiful cathedral of Amiens (1220–1288), pure Gothic found its highest expression; "in dignity inferior to Chartres, in sublimity to Beauvais, in decorative splendour to Rheims, and in loveliness of figure-sculpture to Bourges. It has nothing like the artful pointing and moulding of the arcades of Salisbury —nothing of the might of Durham. And yet, in all, and more than these, ways, outshone or overpowered, the cathedral of Amiens deserves the name given to it by M. Viollet le Duc the 'Parthenon of Gothic Architecture.' "[4]

FIGURE 61 — *Plan of Amiens Cathedral*

As the type of French Gothic, the cathedral of Amiens is contrasted later with that of Salisbury (p. 174).

Almost invariably the French cathedral plan showed a semicircular or apsidal arrangement of the

[4] Ruskin, "The Bible of Amiens."

158

east end. At Laon and Poitiers we find the square end, so general in England; but in the typical plan the east end had a series of radiating chapels, forming a *chevet*— an arrangement already noticed in the Romanesque church of Notre Dame at Clermont, and seen in the illustration of Amiens Cathedral.

The transepts were not so fully developed as with us: Bourges has none, and Notre Dame, Paris, has only rudimentary ones. The main (west) front usually contained a triple portal, and over this ran a frieze of niches filled with royal statues. The superb porches, with elaborately sculptured, deeply recessed archways enriched with "dedicated shapes of saints and kings," are specially characteristic of French design, and form the richest feature of the exterior. In many examples they project a considerable distance in front of the main wall and are roofed with massive gables. Magnificent examples are found at Bourges, Chartres, Amiens and, perhaps finest of all, at Rheims; witness the old couplet—

Clocher de Chartres, nef d'Amiens,
Chœur de Beauvais, portail de Rheims—

which puts before us the popular idea of the four grandest features to be found among the Gothic cathedrals of France.

The French buildings are generally on a vaster and more imposing scale than our English cathedrals. There is no Gothic design on this side of the channel comparable in these respects with the giants at Rheims, Paris, Bourges, Amiens or Chartres, all of which were in course of erection in the early half of the thirteenth

From an Engraving by J. Coney.

FIGURE 61A — *Rheims Cathedral*

century. In respect of length the cathedrals of France did not differ greatly from the English examples, for the longest (Amiens, 450 feet), is exceeded by some of our cathedrals, *e.g.,* Winchester, Ely and York; but they surpassed ours in width and area, and especially in boldness and loftiness of the vaulting.

To the first period belong several monastic buildings, amongst others the picturesque Mont S. Michel, portions of which, however, have been re-built later.

Of the buildings of the Second Period the most noteworthy is the unfinished cathedral of Beauvais. The foundation dates from 1225, but the greater portion of the design of this—the loftiest and slenderest of all French cathedrals—was not carried out until the second half of the thirteenth century. In this design the builders carried the Gothic principles to the extreme limit of daring, and in a few years the slender supports collapsed, and the building required to be almost entirely reconstructed. As it now stands, the height from the pavement to the top of the vaulting is not less than 160 feet! Similar measurements at Ely, a longer cathedral of the English type, give less than 75 feet.

Few cathedrals of the Middle Period were completed, except after long delays, for the enthusiasm had waned. In S. Ouen at Rouen, built between 1320–1350, we have a fine example, with additions of a later date. Limoges (1272) was begun on an extensive scale, but is still incomplete; Toulouse, begun in the same year, was not completed until the sixteenth century; Narbonne is still unfinished. Yet there was no inconsiderable amount of

Drawn by W. Eden Nesfield.

FIGURE 62 — *House of Jacques Cœur, Bourges*

162

building carried on, and many additions were made to the earlier designs which have greatly enhanced their beauty and interest. The great rose-windows, as at Rouen, are features of this period.

Profusion of rich detail and florid elaboration of tracery curves marked the Third, or Flamboyant, Period. Such work is seen in the church of S. Maclou at Rouen; finer still in the rich façade which was added to the older cathedral of Rouen at the beginning of the sixteenth century. In each of these examples may be noticed the striking development of elaborate tracery; the gables over the porches are an open network of stone, suggestive of windows without glass. Notable examples of the flamboyant work are the façades of Troyes and of Tours, the church of S. Jacques at Dieppe, and the Hotel de Ville at Rouen, of the same date as the cathedral front (1500). The florid architecture of the sixteenth century culminated in such fantastic work as the sepulchral church of Brou, in which almost all dignity of composition is frittered away in a dazzling profusion of lace-like carving, marvellous masterpieces of the craftsmen's art—

> Flemish carvers, Lombard gilders,
> German masons, smiths from Spain—

but a decadent form of architecture.

The Gothic spirit in France was not confined to ecclesiastical buildings, but pervaded every branch of secular and domestic architecture. Many a French town, as Troyes, Provins or Bourges, retains fine specimens of the later Gothic house; witness the picturesque house of

Jacques Cœur at Bourges (1443). The more important buildings were of stone; but in shop-fronts and designs on a smaller scale the half-timbered façade, with its overhanging, steep-pitched gables and fully moulded beams and brackets, was more frequently seen. With later domestic buildings details become less distinctly Gothic, but the high gables and steep roofs and other Gothic traditions survived, and, as we shall see, strongly influenced the designs of the French Renaissance builders of the sixteenth and later centuries.

GREAT BRITAIN.—The division of Gothic architecture in England into periods presents some difficulties. Many persons are dissatisfied with the old grouping of Early English or thirteenth century, Decorated or fourteenth, and Perpendicular or fifteenth century. This arrangement suggests a complete change from one period into another at the end of each century. Now, whatever terms be accepted, we must bear in mind that all Gothic building was more or less in a state of transition, and that there was always continuous development. But summer has to be divided from spring and spring from winter at fixed dates, whatever may be the weather at the time; yet wintry incursions into spring are by no means unusual.

Prof. Lethaby[5] has endeavoured with some success to sub-divide the periods, and we quote his thoughtful suggestions here for the reader's benefit.

A transition, leading to Gothic, he points out,

[5] W. R. Lethaby, "Architecture."

is visible in works built about 1150, and the Gothic manner of building lingered on till the middle of the sixteenth century. We may thus give to the Gothic a total period of four centuries. In 1348–50 occurred the Great Plague called the Black Death. From this time later Gothic begins, and it is well to remember the date, 1350, as the key to the chronology of British art. By putting two centuries in front we get 1150, the date of the beginning, and adding two centuries we obtain 1550, for the death date. The four centuries he divides thus:—

1100–1150 Mature Norman.

1150–1200 Transition (from Norman to Gothic).

1200–1250 Lancet.

1250–1300 Geometrical.

1300–1350 Curvilinear.

1350–1400 Late Decorated.

1400–1450 Mature Perpendicular.

1450–1500 Rectilinear.

1500–1550 Tudor.

It is well, however, to avoid too elaborate a terminology, and he suggests that as "the most characteristic phases of the Norman, Early English, Decorated, Perpendicular and Tudor styles fell in the twelfth, thirteenth, fourteenth, fifteenth and sixteenth centuries, these names may stand more exactly for the styles as they were in the first halves of those several centuries." Needless to say, the periods overlapped one another to some extent, and there was no sudden change in the style. The course of architecture throughout the periods was uninterrupted, as we shall see by noting the leading characteristics of each:—

Early English, or Early Thirteenth Century. Long, narrow, lancet-headed windows; angle-buttresses set squarely; deeply undercut mouldings to the arches; slender, detached columns to doors and windows; circular capitals, unfoliated, or with crisp bulbous foliage; clustered piers; little ornament, except the dog-tooth.

FIGURE 63 — *Early English Window, Tinwell, Rutlandshire*

Decorated, or Early Fourteenth Century. Greater richness of detail; buttresses enriched with crockets, niches, etc., and often set obliquely at the angles;

windows wider and more important, and divided by mullions, the upper part filled in with geometrical or (later) elaborate flowing tracery; mouldings shallower and less numerous; carved foliage in the capitals less crisp, with natural forms of oak leaves, etc.; finely carved figures and bosses; *ball-flower* ornament.

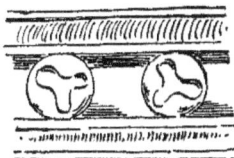

FIGURE 64 — *Ball-flower Ornament*

Perpendicular, or Early Fifteenth Century.—Larger windows with numerous mullions and with vertical tracery carried through to the top of the arch, often intersected by horizontal transomes; almost all wall surfaces panelled, in imitation of the window treatment; doorways frequently finished with a square label over the arch; weak, shallow mouldings; octagonal piers; open timber roofs of elaborate construction, with carved figures of angels. With the later work, *Tudor-rose, portcullis*, and *Fleur de-lys* ornaments.

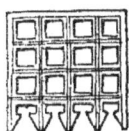

FIGURE 65 — *Portcullis and Tudor-rose Ornaments*

Tudor, or Early Sixteenth Century.—Features similar to the Perpendicular, but more fully developed, or carried to excess; arches flattened at the apex, and struck from four centres; more elaborate vaulting; richly ornamented parapets with battlements. Many important collegiate buildings, mansions and manor houses erected during this century, in the designs of which the Tudor features gradually mingled with and merged into those of the Renaissance.

There was no Gothic cathedral building era in England to compare with the early part of the thirteenth century in France. We have seen that the period following the Norman Conquest had been a very active one, and had covered the island with such ecclesiastical buildings as were unrivalled even in France at that time. These grand structures were sufficient for the people's immediate wants. But as the Gothic tide began to make its presence felt, the new features were gradually introduced into new work which was in progress, and, after a period of transition, began to supplant the sturdy Norman details and the round arch, though there was no wholesale pulling down and rebuilding of cathedral churches, such as was witnessed in France. Thus it comes about that the cathedrals of England are less homogeneous than those of our French neighbours, for, with one or two exceptions, they represent a mixture of styles, and are in reality Norman structures which have been remodelled and enlarged by the Gothic builders.

This fact tended to emphasise a characteristic peculiarity of the English cathedral plan—its remarkable length in proportion to its breadth. The Anglo-Norman builders, probably for constructive reasons, showed a preference for narrow naves; and as it would have been impossible to widen the naves without pulling down the buildings, the subsequent Gothic additions were all in the direction of emphasising the length rather than the width, so that in several of our English plans we find the proportions of length to breadth as great as 7 to 1. At Salisbury, an entirely Gothic building, the dimensions are 450 feet and 78 feet respectively—almost 6 to 1.

The long, narrow naves of the English cathedrals are ill-adapted for a service, or for enabling a congregation to see what was taking place at the altar; but there were compensations, for, as Fergusson points out, "in pictorial effect they surpass everything erected on the Continent, unless with greatly increased dimensions of height or width. Whether, therefore, it were hit upon by accident or design, its beauty was immediately appreciated, and formed the governing principle in the design of all the English cathedrals. It was a discovery which has added more to the sublimity of effect which characterises most of our cathedrals than any other principle introduced during the Middle Ages."

The earliest traces of Gothic in England are found in Norman buildings which were in course of erection during the middle of the twelfth century, *e.g.,* the nave of Rochester cathedral. Pointed arches were introduced at Malmesbury Abbey (1130), and at Kirkstall Abbey (1160), and almost equally early examples of ribbed vaulting are found at Furness Abbey, Worcester Cathedral, and elsewhere. The ideas were no doubt imported from France, but they developed in a different manner, and probably owed much of their development to English architects. It is to Canterbury, however, that we must look for the first application of Gothic on a complete and extensive scale.

Canterbury at this early date had already seen much history. The cathedral had been rebuilt in the tenth century by Odo, but the archbishop appointed by William the Norman, Lanfranc, destroyed the whole of the old building, and rebuilt it on a larger scale in

FIGURE 66 — *Choir, Canterbury Cathedral*

1070. But, like the old Roman emperors, some of the abbot-builders of those days had little respect for their predecessors' work, and within twenty years it was again pulled down, and rebuilt by Ernulph. His successor, Conrad, built it on a more extensive scale, including in his design the "glorious choir of Conrad," the finest work that had been executed in England at that date (1110). When this choir was again destroyed—by fire in 1174—the monks commissioned a Frenchman, William of Sens, to superintend the work of restoration. The new

FIGURE 67 — *Part of Arcade, Canterbury*

choir, designed by him, affords the earliest example of the development of the Gothic style carried out in an important English building and in a complete manner. Four years after the work had been put in hand, William of Sens was killed by a fall from a scaffold, and his place was taken by an English architect, who carried out his predecessor's design with little variation. The new choir, thus completed (1175–1184), bears some resemblance to the cathedral of Sens, and is distinctly French in its plan and details, with an apsidal arrangement of the east end, and a stone vaulted roof.

The difference between the new and the old work—the Gothic of 1175 and the Norman of 1110—is very marked, and may be studied at the point in the arcading where the new abuts against the old. The illustration on the previous page shows the plain, cushion-shaped Norman capital at this point, supporting on the one side the sturdy round arch with its roughly axed zig-zag, on the other the Gothic work with its chiselled mouldings and carved ornament.

The great progress which the art of building had made between these dates is emphasised by Gervase, a contemporary writer, who was an eye-witness of the progress of the work. "The pillars of the old and new work," he says, "were alike in form; but in the old capitals the work was plain, in the new ones exquisite in sculpture. There the arches and everything else was plain, or sculptured with an axe and not with a chisel; but here, almost throughout is appropriate sculpture. No marble columns were there, but here are innumerable ones. There, there was a ceiling of wood, decorated with excellent painting; but here is a vault, beautifully constructed of stone and light tufa." And all this, he wisely remarks, will be better understood by inspection than by any description.

When Gothic had once been used throughout a design of such importance, it soon became generally adopted. In 1185 Hugh of Burgundy was appointed Bishop of Lincoln, and at once set to work on his cathedral, the east end of which—St. Hugh's choir—he rebuilt in pure Gothic style. But in various parts of the country the Norman round arch continued in use, in conjunction with the pointed arch, until the beginning of the thirteenth century, from which period the commencement of the sway of Gothic in England may be said to date.

Within the early years of the century many cathedrals were enlarged in the style, and the period gave us, among others, such works as the magnificent west porch of Ely, the presbytery of Winchester, the choir of Rochester, Fountains Abbey, and the choir of the Temple Church, London. But for the typical church of this date we look to Salisbury (1220–1258), an entirely new foundation, which was designed and built throughout in the Early English,

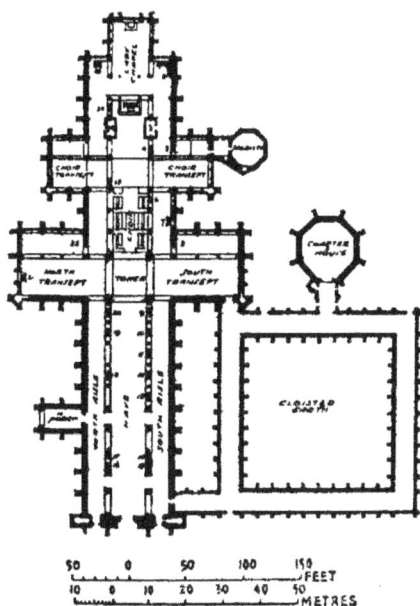

FIGURE 68 — *Plan of Salisbury Cathedral*

or thirteenth century, style. A comparison of this with the plan of a typical French cathedral of the same date, Amiens (p. 158), brings into relief the points of divergence between the English and the French models:—

AMIENS.	SALISBURY.
Proportion of length to breadth, about 3 to 1.	Proportion of length to breadth, about 6 to 1.
Semicircular east end with *chevet*.	Square east end.
Transepts unimportant, with very slight projection.	Double transepts, with deep projection.
Imposing and richly decorated triple west porch.	West porch small, almost mean.
Lofty vaulting (140 feet in height), requiring an elaborate system of flying buttresses for support.	Low vaulting (84 feet), with simple exterior treatment.
Circular rose-window in the west front, and elaborate tracery.	Lancet-headed windows with little tracery.

The central tower, rising above the crossing of the nave and transepts, was a leading feature in the English cathedral design, as at Salisbury, where the spire rises to the height of 424 feet, and dominates the whole design. Such an effect was impossible in the French building, for the lofty vaulting and the high-pitched roof gave such height to the structure that any attempt at a dominating feature was rendered futile by reason of the immense mass of the building. The central flèche of Amiens appears insignificant, yet in height it is almost equal to that of Salisbury, the loftiest of our spires; while the north and south towers, more than 200 feet high, which would add dignity to an English cathedral, hardly rise above the ridge of the roof. The lofty French cathedral, in fact, was designed to be seen from the

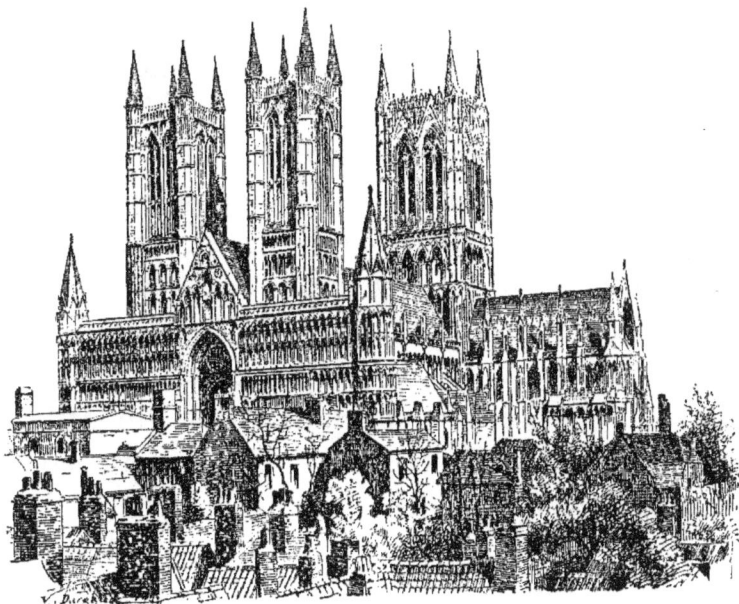

FIGURE 69 — *Lincoln Cathedral*

inside as Ruskin, in his eulogy of French Gothic, and of Amiens cathedral in particular, admitted: "The outside of a French cathedral, except for its sculpture, is always to be thought of as the wrong side of the stuff, in which you find how the threads go that produce the inside or right-side pattern." In England our designs are less ambitious, but there is no "wrong side" to them; and there is something as essentially English about the Cathedral of Lincoln, or the mighty pile of Durham, with its three dominating towers, (PLATE XIX, p. 182) as there is about Wells with its charm and quiet dignity, or Salisbury and its close of—

> Red brick and ashlar long and low,
> With dormers and with oriels lit.

We must not overlook one fact, however, which

further helps to explain the emphatic differences between the French and the English Gothic exteriors. The French building was essentially a cathedral church, the seat of the bishop, who represented the active religious life of the community: it was desirable that his seat, his cathedral church, should be placed in the midst of the busy life of the city, just as would be the case with an important civic building. The English building, on the other hand, was in many cases not primarily a cathedral, but an abbey church, attached to a monastery. The monks, to whom the abbey owed its foundation, sought for their habitation a secluded spot, rather than the busy city, so that they might meditate undisturbed in their cloisters, pray in their church, fish perhaps in their stream. As years went on, the old order changed; but the cathedrals of England, in many of their features, have always retained the impress of these earlier days.

The abbey of Westminster (1245–1271), whose originally quiet surroundings have now given place to the bustle of London life, presents a curious blending of the French and English plans. The nave and deep, square transepts are as thoroughly English in arrangement and detail as the east end, with its *chevet* and apsidal chapels, is French. The unusual height of the vaulting—100 feet—and the consequent development of the flying buttress, are also suggestive of French influence.

Towards the close of the thirteenth century the desire for additional richness and ornamentation brought about a gradual change in the character of the architecture. This was most marked in the treatment of the window openings, which were increased in size and divided into separate lights by mullions, formed in the upper part into geometrical tracery. These geometrical designs soon gave place to lines of double curvature, or flowing tracery, which the English architects treated with great skill, and which became the characteristic feature of the Decorated style during the fourteenth century, culminating magnificently in such works as the west window of York Minster and the east window of Carlisle Cathedral.

FIGURE 70 — *Flowing Tracery,*
Sleaford Church, Lincolnshire

Hand in hand with the increasing importance of the window openings we find, as in France, considerable development in the art of decorative glass-staining. In the fifteenth century the majority of the great church windows of England were filled with richly coloured stained glass, but the iconoclasts of the seventeenth century did their work only too thoroughly. The glass was too "idolatrous" for the taste of the Puritans, and met with no quarter at their hands. A paragraph from the "Petition of the Weamen of Middlesex," in 1641, which bore 12,000 signatures, helps to explain the extraordinary disappearance of most of the glass from our English churches. "We desire," it says, "that prophane glasse windows whose superstitious paint makes many idolaters may be humbled and dashed in pieces against the ground; for our conscious tels us that they are diabolicall and the father of Darknesse was the inventor of them, being the chief Patron to damnable pride."

The change from the graceful window forms of the Decorated to the stiff rectangular lines of the Perpendicular period seems almost like a reaction. Gothic builders at the end of the fourteenth century were seized with the desire to emphasise in every possible way the vertical lines of the design, so that

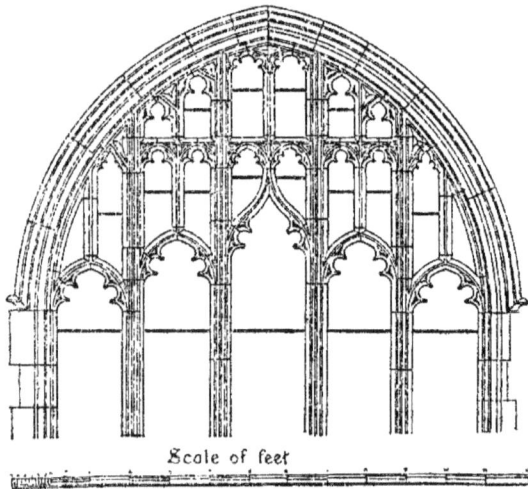

Scale of feet

FIGURE 71 — *Perpendicular Window, Broad-Chalke, Wilts*

the "perpendicular" line became the dominating feature of every detail. The whole wall surface, inside and out, was divided into a series of rectangular panels, and as the enormous windows occupied the whole space at the east and west ends, as well as the wall spaces between the buttresses, they were treated as a series of glazed panels. The exterior of King Henry VII's Chapel at Westminster Abbey is an elaborate example of this method of treatment (PLATE XX, p. 186). Simultaneously with this was developed the beautiful, and essentially English, form of vaulting known as fantracery, familiar to us in the ceilings of King Henry VII's Chapel, Westminster; S. George's Chapel, Windsor; Divinity Schools, Oxford; and the Chapel of King's College, Cambridge (PLATE XVIII, p. 180)—

> That branching roof
> Self-poised and scooped into a thousand cells,
> Where light and shade repose, where music dwells
> Lingering—and wandering on as loth to die.

The chapter-house, which forms a graceful adjunct to many of our cathedrals, is another feature peculiar to English architecture. In Norman times this was rectangular in form, as at Bristol (1155); but shortly after this date, the circular or polygonal plan, with a central column, came into use. The first to adopt this form was the architect of the chapter-house at Worcester, a building which became the recognised type for later designs at Lincoln (1225), Salisbury, Westminster (1250), and Wells (1300). In each of these a central column gives the necessary support to the vaulting of the roof. At York the central pillar has been dispensed

PLATE XVIII — *The Chapel, King's College, Cambridge*

with, and the Gothic ceiling is carried entirely upon the walls of the octagon. The design gains immeasurably by the removal of this support, and the beautiful work almost justifies the builder's inscription:—

Ut Rosa flos florum,
Sic Domus ista Domorum.

The ceiling, in the form of a dome, is beautiful in detail, but executed in wood.

FIGURE 72 — *View of Interior, Chapter House, York*

Cathedral building did not monopolise the attention of our architects, as it did in France. A most complete record of the progress of Gothic is to be found in the beautiful parish churches which are scattered over all parts of the island. Many of these show a beauty and variety of detail equal to the foremost of the cathedrals. All periods are represented, but the churches of the

PLATE XIX — *Durham Cathedral*

fourteenth and fifteenth centuries abound with the finest examples. The typical English church plan has a nave with side aisles and a clerestory, a long, narrow chancel with square east end, west tower, and south doorway. The most important churches, as those of Boston, Grantham, Coventry, etc., almost rivalled the cathedrals in dimensions. and frequently had a south door enriched with a vaulted porch, with a library or other rooms over it.

Except on a small scale, as in these porches, or in isolated instances, vaulted ceilings were not found in the parish churches. Instead of them we find open timber roofs, treated with remarkable ingenuity, and often with great elaboration. By means of a skilful development of roof-truss the outward thrust of the ceiling against the walls was reduced to a minimum; the roof was thus easily carried and the exterior design was not hampered by structural difficulties. The trusses and brackets were richly moulded, and the ceiling spaces treated in a highly decorative manner. Fine examples of these roofs are found in the Perpendicular churches of Norfolk, and in the halls of many of the colleges of Oxford and Cambridge, notably that of Christ Church, Oxford. Largest and most famous of all is the great roof of Westminster Hall, London (1397), covering a space 239 feet in length by 68 feet in width. Characteristic work is found too in many of the old castles, as in the castle, or fortified Manor House, of Stokesay, in Shropshire, with its later Elizabethan half-timbered gatehouse.

From a drawing by Arthur Keen.

FIGURE 73 — *Stokesay Castle, Shropshire*

There are few fields of study more full of interest than these buildings, or than the old parish churches of England. Much history which would otherwise have been lost may be found written upon church walls by those who have eyes to see it; nor is more than a slight acquaintance with the characteristic features of each period necessary to enable the student to read the history and to assign a date to the construction of the work. In distinguishing the periods, all mouldings and ornaments are of very great value. Mouldings of the

FIGURE 75 —
Unfoliated Early English Capital, Salisbury

thirteenth century were seldom decorated with any ornament other than the dog-tooth, which took the place of the axed zig-zag of the Normans. The bold, undercut mouldings gave strong effects of light and shade, and required little enrichment; the unfoliated moulded capital is characteristic of Early English architecture; where carved foliage was used it was crisp, bulbous, treated conventionally, and curved boldly outwards, appearing to grow out of the surface. The mouldings of the Decorated period were less defined, and were seldom undercut; the foliage was naturalistic, representing oak and vine leaves, or sea-weed, and the ball-flower supplanted the dogtooth ornament. In

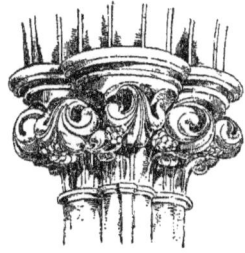

FIGURE 76 — *Foliated Early English Capital, Hereford*

Perpendicular work the Tudor-rose, portcullis, and fleur-de-lys appear as ornaments upon richly panelled wall-surfaces; mouldings were wide and shallow, and of secondary importance. In Norfolk and Suffolk the panels on the exterior wall surfaces were frequently filled in with flint work. Wooden screens with elaborate tracery shut off the chancel.

FIGURE 74 — *A Perpendicular Church, Outwell, Norfolk*

PLATE XX — *Chapel of King Henry VII, Westminster Abbey*

In striking contrast to later times is the almost entire absence of municipal buildings throughout the four centuries succeeding the Norman conquest: "the king, the baron, and the bishop were the estates of the realm; the people were nowhere," and neither municipalities nor guilds could assert an independent existence.

In addition to the buildings mentioned above, the following are good examples of the respective styles:—

EARLY ENGLISH

Temple Church, London . . . . East End.
Westminster Abbey . . . . East End, Transepts,
                               etc.
Fountains Abbey
York Cathedral . . . . Transepts.
Ely Cathedral . . . . Choir and Transepts.
Wells Cathedral . . . . Nave & West Front.
Peterborough Cathedral . . . . West Front.

DECORATED

Ely Cathedral . . . . Lady Chapel and
                               Lantern.
York Cathedral . . . . Choir and Chapter
                               House.
Merton College Chapel, Oxford . . . . Choir.
Stone Church, Kent.
Lichfield Cathedral . . . . Nave.

PERPENDICULAR

Westminster Hall.
Gloucester Cathedral . . . . Choir & West Front.
Sherborne Minster.
Winchester Cathedral . . . . West Front & Nave.
Magdalen College, Oxford.
Beauchamp Chapel, Warwick.

TUDOR

Henry VII's Chapel, Westminster.
Parts of Hampton Court Palace.
Sutton Place, Guildford.
Compton Wynyates, Warwickshire.
Many Colleges at Oxford and Cambridge.

ITALY.—Gothic architecture, from causes which are not far to seek, never took deep root in Italy. In the first place the style was utterly unsuited to the brilliant climate of a country where it seemed "always afternoon." The Italian regarded his church as a cool resort from the eternal glare of the sun; and the small windows of the basilica, with its grateful gloom, were more to his liking than the "walls of glass" of the style in vogue amongst his neighbours. Again, from the time of the Roman empire, classical tradition had been very strong throughout the country, and had permeated its architecture. The Italian was familiar with, and justly proud of, the classical forms of Rome, upon which the architecture of Western Europe had been modelled. The works of his ancestors, the Romans, had been marked by breadth, solidity, simplicity of parts and by emphatic treatment of horizontal lines; it was hardly to be expected that the narrow, lofty aisles, the multiplicity of vertical lines and mouldings, and the minuteness of detail of the Gothic builders should find favour with him. Moreover, the scientific principles of Gothic construction did not appeal to him, for the mediæval Italian was never a constructive designer. He relied for interior effect upon large unbroken wall surfaces, which were decorated with frescoes or mosaics, or veneered with rich and rare marbles.

When Gothic was introduced, therefore, it was received as a foreign or imported style, which was grafted upon the older forms, with the result that Italian Gothic never divested itself of the influence of Roman traditions. It owed its introduction to the mendicant monks, whose travels brought them into contact with the outer civilisation. Many of the earliest and largest churches were built by these monks—Dominicans or Franciscans. S. Francis of Assisi, the founder of the Franciscans, died in 1226, and the church which enshrined his body was one of the most remarkable examples of Italian Gothic, as well as one of the earliest. Although designed by a German architect, the church of S. Francesco at Assisi (1228–1253) shows strong Italian influence in its composition. Internally the architecture is quite subordinate to the decorative paintings, for which the wall spaces were intended, and with which they have been filled. The church is built in two stories: in the lower church the vaulting over the high altar is enriched with frescoes by Giotto; so small, however, are the window-openings, and so dim the light, that it is not possible to appreciate fully the detail of the paintings, unless it be for an hour or two on the brightest days.

S. Francesco contains the shrine of S. Francis. His followers, the Franciscans, and the Dominican brotherhood (founded 1216), were responsible for many of the earliest and most important Gothic churches, including S. Francesco at Bologna, the Church of the Frari at Venice, S. Anastasia at Verona, S. Maria Novella at Florence, and S. Maria sopra Minerva (1280), the only important Gothic church in Rome.

The most successful examples of the style in Italy are the cathedrals, built upon an imposing scale, and showing, in almost every instance, the peculiarities of the Italian treatment of Gothic:—Milan (1385–1418), the largest of all mediæval churches except Seville; Siena (1243), Orvieto (1290), Florence (1294), Ferrara, and the church of S. Petronio, Bologna (1390), projected upon a vaster scale than the cathedral of Milan, but never completed. In some of these designs there is little, with the exception of the details, to distinguish them from the earlier Romanesque buildings. At Siena and Orvieto the round arch is freely used, while a striking interior effect is gained by the use of alternate bands of black and white marbles. The façade in each case is a rich composition of coloured marbles with three gables, and a deeply recessed triple porch, enriched, at Orvieto, with gorgous mosaics. The love of the Italians for colour

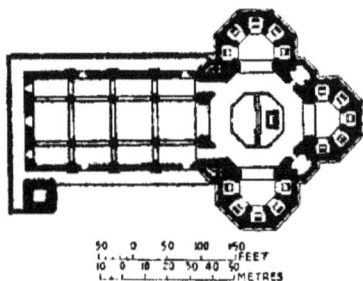

FIGURE 77 — *Plan of the Duomo, Florence*

decoration in preference to the brilliancy of stained glass finds expression at Orvieto, where small window-openings are filled with slabs of rich translucent alabaster.

The cathedral of Florence, begun in 1294 by Arnolfo del Cambio, was not completed until the fifteenth century, when the dome was added by Brunelleschi.

PLATE XXII — *The Dome, Florence Cathedral*

Here everything is on a colossal scale; but the architect made the mistake of thinking that largeness of parts would invest the whole with dignity and grandeur. The vast nave, which, in a French design of similar importance, would have been subdivided into ten or twelve bays, is here spanned by four great arches, which are left bare, with hardly a moulding or a vestige of detail to give scale to the composition. The walls above are bare and colourless and—save for the beautiful glass—cannot fail to disappoint. Of the dome we shall speak later, when dealing with the architecture of the Renaissance.

In direct contrast to the Duomo at Florence is the remarkable cathedral at Milan, bewildering in the multiplicity of its parts and the elaboration of its detail. The exterior design is lost in a perfect forest of pinnacles, decorated with rich and intricate tracery,—

A mount of marble, a hundred spires!

In the interior a belt of niches, filled with statuary, crowns the nave-piers, in place of the usual capitals. The ceiling is painted in imitation of elaborate fan-tracery.

Milan Cathedral (1385–1418) was one of the latest of the important Gothic buildings erected in Italy, but the style was still regarded as a foreign importation, and had not become, in any sense, a national one. In proof of this we find, within a few miles of Milan, a building contemporary with the cathedral, yet dissimilar in every feature and showing very little true Gothic influence. The famous Carthusian monastery, or Certosa, at Pavia, begun in 1396, was built entirely of brick and terra-cotta. Here the vaulting is Gothic, but in other respects the external design, with its picturesquely grouped turrets, round arches, and arcaded galleries, is thoroughly Romanesque in character. The marble façade is a Renaissance addition.

The Italians, as we have seen, were great decorators rather than constructors, and Gothic art found natural expression in small decorative works such as porches and tombs, or in secular monuments. The porch of S. Maria Maggiore at Bergamo is a characteristic specimen of this work—fascinating in its clothing of Gothic detail, yet built up in so unscientific a manner as to rely for security upon a system of iron ties and clamps. And here it may be mentioned that the use of iron tie-rods, which was almost universal in Italy, indicates that the builders did not appreciate the true principles of thrust and counter-thrust, which were the essence of Gothic construction. No doubt this lack of constructive genius hampered them in their more important designs, so that we must look to decorative works, such as the tombs of the Scaligers at Verona, for the purest expression of Gothic feeling. Giotto's campanile, adjoining the cathedral at Florence, is another beautiful example of Italian decorative Gothic. The smooth wall surfaces are entirely faced with panelling of coloured marbles, much of it delicately sculptured in low relief, and the windows are unsurpassed for their exquisite detail and grace; but there is no Gothic backbone in the design.

The civic life and enterprise of the great mediæval towns in Italy were reflected in their municipal buildings. Cities, forming independent principalities, were constantly at war with one another, or with themselves, and the town-hall of necessity partook of the character of a fortress. Elegance was sacrificed to security, and few features were introduced, save the lofty tower and the frowning cornice, each of which fulfilled a definite purpose; yet there are few more delightful and expressive designs than the Palazzo Vecchio, Florence (1298); or the Palazzo Pubblico, Siena (1290) with its slender and graceful Mangia Tower. In Venice alone, all-powerful, and therefore peaceful, the architect was able to give full play to his fancy, and produced examples of domestic Gothic art unrivalled in any country in Europe. Carrying on an extensive trade with Byzantium and with many Eastern ports, Venice developed a unique style in which much of the Byzantine grace and richness were blended with the Gothic details of the West, and which found its highest expression in the remarkable Doges' Palace (1354) adjoining the church of S. Mark, "the centre of the most beautiful architectural group that adorns any city of Europe, or of the world." The design (PLATE XXIII, opposite), with its double story of arcades and traceried arches, is familiar, from illustrations and photographs, to readers in all parts of the world, and has received added fame from the loving pen of Ruskin, to whom it represented "a model of all perfection." "The front of the Doges' Palace," he writes, "is the purest and most chaste model that I can name (but one) of the fit application of colour to public buildings. The sculpture and mouldings are all white; but the wall

PLATE XXIII — *Doges' Palace, Venice*

PLATE XXIII — *Foscari Palace, Venice*

surface is chequered with marble blocks of pale rose, the chequers being in no wise harmonised, or fitted to the forms of the windows; but looking as if the surface had been completed first, and the windows cut out of it. . . . It would be impossible, I believe, to invent a more magnificent arrangement of all that is in building most dignified and most fair."

Many choice examples of Venetian Gothic are found along the banks of the Canal, none more beautiful than the refined and ornate Cà d'Oro, and the Pisani and Foscari Palaces (PLATE XXIII, opposite).

GERMANY.—In Germany Gothic architecture was borrowed directly from France. Its development was irregular, and the style, with one or two exceptions, produced nothing to equal the fine Romanesque churches of the earlier centuries. For many years after its introduction it was merely grafted upon the Romanesque stem,—a fusion of styles which is seen in Magdeburg Cathedral (begun 1210), constructed on the massive lines of the twelfth-century churches, and clothed with the more graceful Gothic details. A little later, in the church of S. Elizabeth at Marburg (1250), we find an essentially German type of building, the "hall-church," in which the clerestory of the nave disappears, and the side aisles are raised to the same height as the nave.

Strasbourg Cathedral, designed by the Germans upon French lines, has a rich façade, and a large rose-window in the west gable. The magnificent cathedral at Cologne, finest of all, is an enlarged edition of a

French plan, differing little from that of Amiens, but with double aisles to the nave. The work of building this cathedral was carried on very slowly. Begun in 1248, the choir was completed in 1322, and the remaining works, after being proceeded with intermittently, were entirely suspended until the middle of the nineteenth century. The nave, aisle, and transepts were completed, from the original designs, in 1848, and in 1863 the church was complete in all respects, with the exception of the great Western spires, 500 feet high, which were added in 1880. The style is uniform throughout, but the later details lack the vigour of thirteenth-century Gothic.

FIGURE 78 — *Strasbourg Cathedral*

Cologne is the largest of all mediæval cathedrals, with the exception of Seville and Milan.

Fine examples of German Gothic are found among the town-halls, e.g., Ratisbon, Brunswick and Breslau.

BELGIUM, SPAIN, ETC.—In Belgium the most important church of the period was the cathedral at Antwerp (1360), with a remarkable plan, showing three aisles upon each side of the nave, and a total width of 160 feet, equal to one-half the entire length of the building. The florid west front (fifteenth century) is a rich example of the later Flemish treatment. Other cathedrals of interest were found—before the desecration of Belgium by the Germans—at Bruges, Ypres, Ghent, Liege and Louvain, all showing the influence of France. It was in the municipal buildings, however, that the new style became more thoroughly nationalised. Belgium has some famous examples of trade-halls and town-halls, erected by the burghers during the most prosperous period of their cities' history. The cloth-halls at Ypres (shown in the Frontispiece) and Ghent, and the town-halls of Brussels, Ghent, Bruges and Louvain are—or were—notable examples. The rich façades are treated somewhat floridly in the manner of the fifteenth-century Gothic, and are surmounted by a steep roof, broken by several stories of dormer windows. A lofty tower generally forms part of the design.

In Spain, the earliest Gothic churches were the Cathedrals of Burgos (1230) and Toledo (1227): these and others show the influence of French examples. At Barcelona and Gerona internal buttresses take the thrust of the vaults, as they do at Albi in France. Seville Cathedral (1401–1520), the largest of all mediæval churches, was built upon the site of a Moorish mosque of similar dimensions, a fact which explains the peculiarity of its plan—a huge rectangle, with square east end, measuring 415 feet by 298 feet, and covering an area of 124,000 feet.

CHAPTER VIII

RENAISSANCE ARCHITECTURE

In the preceding chapter we have seen that classical tradition—derived from the days of the Roman empire—was too strong in Italy to allow the principles of Gothic to be received there with any degree of favour. The Italian never ceased to look upon the style as a foreign, or imported one. The very name with which they branded it, "Gothic," which has now lost its original meaning, was intended to distinguish the "barbarous" style from their own national architecture. When the Gothic style was used, it was so modified by the Italian architect that many of its characteristic features quite disappeared. As an example, the great cathedral at Florence was noted, in which the nave was divided into four colossal bays, each with a span of almost 60 feet. The designer did not realise that these classical ideas of spaciousness and largeness of parts were fatal when applied to Gothic designs.

Yet Arnolfo del Cambio, the architect of the cathedral of Florence, was one of the greatest builders of the Middle Ages. "No Italian architect has enjoyed the proud privilege of stamping his own individuality more strongly on his native city than Arnolfo. When we take our stand upon the hill of Samminiato, the Florence at our feet owes her physiognomy in a great measure to this man. The tall tower of the Palazzo Vecchio, the bulk of the Duomo, and the long, oblong mass of S. Croce, are all his. Giotto's campanile, Brunelleschi's cupola on the dome, and the church of Orsammichele, though not designed by him, are all placed where he had planned."[6]

Arnolfo's plan of the cathedral embraced a huge dome—a classical feature—to be carried upon an octagon, 143 feet in diameter; but he died before the dome, as he had designed it, could be constructed, and he left behind him no information as to the method he had intended to adopt for covering the octagon. Nothing further was done until, in 1417, as the result of a public competition, the task of constructing the dome was intrusted to a young competitor named Brunelleschi. Now, the story of Brunelleschi is the story of the origin and growth of Renaissance architecture in Italy.

The Renaissance, or revival of classical forms in art and literature, was the result of a great national and intellectual movement which manifested itself in Italy during the fourteenth century, and thence spread over the whole of Western Europe. Many causes contributed to the revival:—the fashion, which became general, of reading and studying the ancient Greek and Latin authors; the existence, in Italy, of old classical monuments, from which the styles and details might be studied; the inherited classical tradition; perhaps,

[6] Symonds, "The Renaissance in Italy."

too, the asceticism of the Middle Ages, against which the freedom of the Renaissance was a reaction. Added to this, the Gothic style of architecture, which builders were endeavouring to introduce into Italy, was, as we have seen, unpopular, and unsuitable to the brilliant Italian climate.

These conditions gave Brunelleschi his opportunity. At the age of twenty-two he had unsuccessfully competed with Ghiberti for the great bronze doors of the Baptistery. Having left Florence after this, with his friend Donatello, he made his way to Rome, where he worked as a goldsmith, giving all his spare time to the study of the architecture of the old Roman empire, in an endeavour to grasp the true principles of the classical style. On his return to Florence his mind was full of the great scheme for completing the Duomo, which, though it had been in course of erection for more than 110 years, was still unfinished. Amongst those in authority there was much difference of opinion as to the best manner of covering the great octagon and the apses. It was not, as we have said, until 1417 that the council was held in Florence which definitely settled this great question, when the competitors submitted some extraordinary schemes. One advised that the dome should be supported by a central pillar; another suggestion, which seemed to find favour, was that the space over which the dome was to be built should be covered with a huge mound of earth. Coins were to be mixed with the earth, so that the people—after the dome was complete—might be willing to remove the soil from the site for the sake of the money they would find in it! Brunelleschi appears to have been the only architect who felt confident of being able to construct the dome without the use of internal supports, and the work was accordingly intrusted to him; but so little confidence had the authorities in him that they appointed Ghiberti—his successful rival of the bronze doors, who knew nothing of architectural construction—to be his colleague. Ghiberti was quite unfitted for the task, and Brunelleschi made many un-successful attempts to get rid of his partner. Vasari amusingly describes his last, successful ruse:

"One morning," he says, "Filippo [that is, Brunelleschi], instead of appearing at work, stayed in bed, and calling for hot fomentations, pretended to have a severe pain in his side. When the workmen heard of this, while they waited to know what they were to do that day, they asked Ghiberti, what was the next thing? He answered that it was Filippo who arranged all that, and that they must wait for him. 'But do you not know his mind?' they asked. 'Yes,' said Ghiberti, 'but I will do nothing without him.' And this he said to cover himself; for not having seen Filippo's model, and never having asked of him how he meant to conduct the work (for fear of appearing ignorant), he was now obliged to remain inactive. This lasted two days, and the workmen at last betook themselves to the Commissioners who provided the materials, asking what they were to do. 'You have Ghiberti,' was the reply; 'let him exert himself a little.' The Commissioners then went to see Filippo, and having condoled with him in his illness, told him of the harm which his absence was causing to the work. 'Is not Ghiberti there?' he asked passionately. 'Why does not he do something?' 'He does not wish to do anything without you.' 'I could do very well without him,' said Filippo. The hint was not taken, however, for Ghiberti continued to draw his salary, without doing any work, although his removal was promised.

"Filippo then tried another expedient. He presented himself before the Commissioners, and addressed them as follows: 'The sickness which has now passed,' he said, 'might have taken away my life, and stopped this work: therefore if it ever happened that I got ill again, or Ghiberti—whom God preserve!—it would be better that one or the other should continue his own work: therefore I have concluded that, as your excellencies have divided the salary, it would be as well to divide the labour, that each of us, being thus stimulated to show how much he knows, may be honourable and useful to the Republic. There are two difficult things to be done—the bridges upon which the masons must stand, and the chain which is to bind together the eight sides of the cupola. Let Ghiberti take one of them, and I will take the other, that no more time be lost.' "

This arrangement settled Ghiberti. He took in hand the chain, but could make nothing of it, and was at last removed from the works.

Great difficulties were experienced in the construction of the dome, and the work was frequently delayed in progress, so that, in the words of an old writer, the vain Florentines considered that "the heavens were jealous of their dome, which bade fair to rival the beauty of the blue ethereal vault itself." It was completed in 1434, the lantern being added in 1462, after Brunelleschi's death (PLATE XXII, p. 191).

While the dome was in hand Brunelleschi carried out several smaller works in Florence, which had considerable influence with his contemporaries, and turned their thoughts in the direction of the new style. One of the most delightful examples is the Pazzi Chapel (1420) of S. Croce, perhaps the earliest building

From a drawing by C. B. Hutchinson.

FIGURE 79 — *Pazzi Chapel, Florence*

completed in the Renaissance style. Other well-known churches of his are S. Lorenzo and S. Spirito, each of which has a small dome over the crossing of the nave and transepts. All the details are copied from the Roman models, with which careful study had made him familiar.

The second great exponent of Renaissance architecture in Florence was Alberti (1404–1473), who was a young man while Brunelleschi's dome was swelling out against the sky. Alberti was an ardent scholar, and the author of a valuable treatise on the art of building, a book which was, perhaps, the most important work of his life, for it became very popular, and greatly influenced the designs of his contemporaries and successors. Brunelleschi, as we have seen, had made a careful study of the imperial architecture of Rome, but in his own designs he in no way reproduced it. He merely borrowed the great leading principles of Roman construction, and carried out the designs in accordance with his own ideas. Alberti was different: he was pre-eminently a scholar, and had a distinct leaning towards everything Latin. Even his great work was written in Latin, and his partiality for pure Roman details and models is evident in his buildings. In his Ruccelai Palace at Florence, for example (1460), we see the first instance of pilasters applied to the façade; these are introduced into each story (as in the Colosseum), the orders being superimposed, and each carrying an entablature.

Another important work by Alberti was the façade of S. Maria Novella in Florence—an applied-marble facing, in which he introduced pilasters and

FIGURE 79A — *S. Maria Novella, Florence*

a true classical pediment. In this church we see the earliest instance of the use of volutes for connecting the higher walls of the nave with those of the aisles, a feature which was constantly imitated by later designers. The treatment of the church façade was one of the most difficult problems which the early Renaissance architects had to solve, and in many of the churches no attempt was made to solve it. The problem was a new one, for the architects could get no help from the ruins of the baths, theatres, or temples, but found it necessary to invent their own façades and to clothe them with classical details. The result was a lack of sincerity, for the external casing had no structural connection with the building which it was designed to mask.

The churches of S. Andrea at Mantua and S. Francesco at Rimini are important works by Alberti. The latter is worthy of careful study as an illustration of the methods of the Renaissance. In this instance the Gothic church was entirely remodelled, and was dressed up with a profusion of classical detail and ornament. Alberti's incomplete work, while very beautiful, exposes the falsity of principles of the Renaissance methods: there was a tendency among the builders to disregard "that only law, that Use be suggester of Beauty," and at Rimini this fact is borne home upon the visitor. The pilasters, architraves, and other classical features with which Alberti has clothed the interior are merely a series of surface deceits, having nothing more to do with the structural strength of the design than the paintings upon the walls.

Architecture at this period was having a great time at Florence under the patronage of Cosmo de' Medici, a nobleman of vast influence and more than regal wealth. Under Brunelleschi's lead there soon sprang up a band of architects imbued with the same spirit, whose genius created those magnificent monuments of the Renaissance—the Florentine palaces. Chief among these are the Riccardi (1430) by Michelozzo, the Strozzi (1489–1553) by Cronaca, and the Palazzi Antinori, Guadagni, and Pandolfini, the latter from a design by Raphael. These are all characterised by solidity and strength, for they required to be fortresses as well as palaces: the walls were of masonry, in large blocks, heavily "rusticated." In this rustic work, as it is inaptly named, a deep channelling marks the joints, from which the face of the rough stonework projects boldly. In some cases the rustication extends over the whole façade, but it was generally confined to the lower story. This treatment gives a pleasing variation of light and shade, suggesting at the same time a note of sturdiness which is in harmony with the spirit and temper of mediæval Florence.

In the Palazzo Strozzi, which is a good type of the Florentine palace, the rustication is treated simply, but covers the whole façade. A serious defect in the design of many of these buildings is apparent here—the uniform height of the stories, as indicated by the string-courses at the level of the window-sills. This, together with the somewhat monotonous repetition of uniform windows, tends to detract from the grandeur of the design. To some extent the defect is redeemed by the great, finely proportioned cornice, which crowns the building, and makes every other feature subordinate and of secondary importance.

These heavy walls and narrow windows reflect the disturbed civic life of this great republic. The torch-rests of wrought metal, the dim courts, and the gloomy entrances, all tell their own history; in them we trace the habits of caution which, of necessity, characterised the Florentine leaders. And as designs they must be studied, and their merits weighed, amidst their own sunny surroundings, and in connection with the history which they helped to make; for it is impossible to judge them from their reproductions in the form of West-end clubs in sunless London. Seen in Florence, these buildings are great pages of history, which he who passes may read. Fitness is indeed one of the elements of true architecture, and few buildings can lay greater claim than

FIGURE 80 — *Renaissance Capital*

these to represent the fit expression and the embodiment of the spirit of the times which produced them.

In Florence many of the architects of the fifteenth century were trained in the workshops of the craftsmen—rooms in which were carried on, under one roof, the arts of the painter, the goldsmith, and the sculptor. By these craftsmen the new details were developed in decorative accessories, such as altars, pulpits, and monuments, in many of which the work is most delicate and refined; indeed, in many cases, the subordinate architectural works are artistically much finer than the buildings in which they are placed. These details were invariably worked in marble, with delicate mouldings, and exquisite carving in low relief. The pulpit of S. Croce in Florence is a fine example—beautiful in form, and in the execution of every detail.

FIGURE 81 — *S. Maria delle Grazie, Milan*

Great activity in building prevailed in other cities of Italy, outside Florence, during the fifteenth century, and notably in Milan and Venice. Rome at the earlier period was almost entirely dependent upon second-rate Florentine artists, and much of the work there was unimportant.

Milan was the first of the cities in which the new architecture took root; and here, for the first time, we come into contact with the third great Renaissance architect, Bramante, whose work eventually culminated in the great design of S. Peter's in Rome.

Bramante was not born until 1444, when many of the great Florentine buildings which we have noticed were already in existence. Like his nephew, the great Raphael, he was a native of the small town of Urbino. His chief works were in Rome, but among his buildings in Milan may be mentioned a considerable portion of the church of S. Maria delle Grazie, and the little octagonal sacristy of S. Maria presso San Satiro.

The most interesting example of the Renaissance style near Milan is to be found at Pavia, where, in 1491, a façade was added to the Certosa, or monastery. This front is covered with a profusion of marble ornament, richly and delicately wrought, like the ivory carving of a casket, but quite inappropriate for its position.

The Renaissance movement in Milan was about half a century later than in Florence, having, in fact, been introduced there by Florentine artists. In Venice the style was still later in appearing. The Venetians at this period were well satisfied with their architecture, and well they might be, for, as we have seen, the Gothic style, tinged and enriched by Byzantine influences, had produced buildings of exquisite beauty and design. The security and prosperity of the city rendered such fortress-like architecture as that of Florence unnecessary; moreover, there was a state of war between the Florentines and the Venetians, and the two cities hated one another cordially. It is not surprising, then, that Venice should be slow to borrow her forms of architecture from her neighbour. She adopted the style somewhat reluctantly; at first in small details, grafted upon the Gothic forms, as in the Porta della Carta of the Doges' Palace. The design of this gateway is wholly Gothic in composition, but the mouldings, and the sportive Cupids appearing amidst the foliage, are classical suggestions. In the internal quadrangle the Renaissance forms are more evident, mingled with the Gothic pointed arches.

In the delightful little church of S. Maria dei Miracoli, one of the earliest examples of the new style, we see the influence of Byzantine tradition. This influence is suggested, externally, in the cupola and the semi-circular roof and pediment, all of which would seem to be borrowed from the neighbouring S. Mark's. Inside, the walls are incrusted with an inlay of coloured marbles. The façades of the school of S. Mark, and of S. Zaccaria, show features manifestly borrowed from the same source.

Under the strong influences of the Byzantine, and of the characteristic Venetian Gothic, we find, as would be expected, a great divergence from the Florentine model in the Renaissance palaces, which are chiefly found along the banks of the "finest curved street in the world," the Grand Canal. The Spinelli Palace is a good type of the Venetian building. Here the façade has three well-defined stories, crowned by a fine cornice. The lowest story has a central door, with steps leading down to the canal; on the first, or principal, floor is a balcony, an almost indispensable adjunct. The windows are grouped irregularly, in a manner common to most Venetian palaces, the central ones being massed together, while those on either side stand free—a notable improvement upon the monotonous spacing of the Florentine and

FIGURE 82 — *Spinelli Palace, Venice*

215

PLATE XXI — *Courtyard of Cancelleria Palace, Rome*

Roman palaces. The Vendramini Palace (1481) shows similar features.

Rome during the greater part of the fifteenth century was stagnating, and Renaissance architecture made practically no headway there. But in the first half of the sixteenth century so great an impetus was given to the Renaissance movement that this short period witnessed its culmination in the city. The causes which contributed chiefly to this result were the succession of the strong and ambitious Julius II to the Papal chair, and, with his accession, the great increase in wealth and power of the Church in Rome. Wealthy families, whom the troublous times of the preceding century had driven out, returned to the city, and soon began to vie with one another in palace-building. Among the architects the new style found a great exponent in Bramante, who became to Rome what Brunelleschi had been to Florence.

Bramante appears not to have been an especially original genius; but he had, before coming to Rome, the advantage of profiting by the originality of his predecessors in Florence and Milan. His work is marked by great variety of treatment, and, in general, by simplicity and good proportions. One of his earliest designs, the Palazzo Cancellaria, has a simple façade rather monotonously treated, with strips of pilasters spaced in pairs between the windows. The arcading of the courtyard shows a composition of arches and columns, borrowed from the Florentine architects, which became popular with later Renaissance builders (Plate XXI, opposite).

These columns, by-the-bye, like so many other details of Roman buildings, have a strange history. They are monolithic shafts, and originally formed part of the great theatre of Pompey—the first stone theatre of Rome, built about 55 B.C. During the Middle Ages that building suffered the usual fate, and was used as a quarry for stone and marble, from which the basilican church of S. Lorenzo was almost entirely built. Bramante pulled down the greater portion of the basilica, in order to build the great Cancellaria palace for Cardinal Riario, using, amongst other materials, fifty of the old columns for his two-storied arcade.

Bramante's work culminated later in the great design of S. Peter's. Julius II had employed Michelangelo to design a colossal monument for himself, and the ambitious pope next set his mind upon the erection of a vast mausoleum to cover the monument. Bramante was intrusted with the work, and began his great task in 1506. His design took the form of a Greek cross—a cross with four equal arms—with an apsidal end to each arm, and a dome over the crossing.

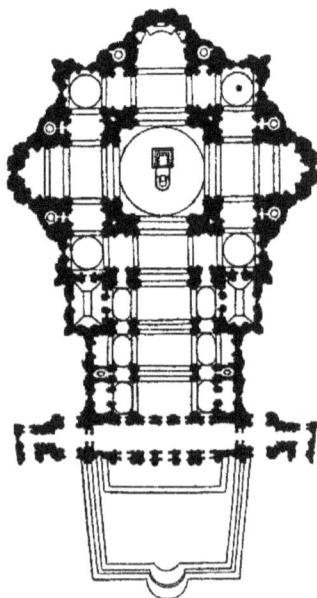

FIGURE 83 — *Plan of S. Peter's, Rome*

The haste with which the work was carried on led to a collapse of some of the main walls, a catastrophe which was followed by Bramante's death in 1514. After this the original design underwent many variations in the hands of a succession of architects—Raphael the painter, Giuliano da San Gallo, and Peruzzi, among others. Each of these devised a new plan and made fundamental alterations to the original scheme, so that little real progress was made with the structure for many years. At last, after a chequered career, the building was handed over in 1546 to Michelangelo, then more than seventy years of age. Under his energetic control the work progressed without interruption for eighteen years. He reverted, in the essentials, to the original plan of Bramante, a Greek cross, but with a square projecting portico to the front, and with the mighty dome over the crossing. With such energy did he prosecute the work that, at his death in 1564, the design was completed, with the exception of the east front and the dome covering. He left behind him a complete model of all the unfinished parts, which were completed under Vignola, Giacomo della Porta, and Fontana, before the end of the century.

So far, the design of Michelangelo, based upon that of Bramante, had been adhered to with little variation: but in the seventeenth century Maderna, the architect to Pope Paul V, set himself the task of improving upon it. He added two bays to the nave,—thus transforming the plan from a Greek into a Latin cross, and destroying the proportions,—and he erected the existing tasteless façade, which completely shuts off the view of the dome from the front. The imposing colonnade, which encircles the piazza, was added later by Bernini (1629–1667).

S. Peter's, thus completed after an interval of 160 years, is the largest church in existence. The vast central aisle, nave, and choir, almost 600 feet in length, are divided into only six bays; the nave itself has four bays only. Over the crossing of the transepts hangs the great dome, 140 feet in diameter, rising to a height of 400 feet. With so few parts, in a building of such colossal dimensions, it follows that all the parts must themselves be on a vast scale. Internally there is nothing to give scale to the building, and to enable the eye to form an estimate of the size; there is no multiplicity of parts, as in a Gothic design, to confuse the eye, and so increase the *apparent* size. Herein lies a serious defect in the design. "Rome disappoints me much; S. Peter's, perhaps, in especial," wrote Clough, and this impression of S. Peter's must be shared by almost every visitor, for the colossal scale of the interior, in the absence of smaller details, is lost upon the observer. Externally, the façade is ruined by the clumsy work of Maderna; but from a distant point of view the mighty dome, dwarfing all other buildings, and seemingly suspended in mid-air, is an impression that can never be forgotten. "There's a kind of miracle in it. Go where you will, that dome follows you. Again and again, storm and mist may blot out the rest—that remains." And it is perhaps only in this dim, blue distance, when one is enabled to contrast the great mass with the surrounding buildings, that the mind can fully gauge the immensity of this great work of Michelangelo.

The story of the building of S. Peter's carries us down to the seventeenth century. During the 150 years that the work was in progress, Renaissance architecture passed through various phases. In the middle of the sixteenth century a treatise by Vignola upon the classical orders had great influence upon his contemporaries, and led to a more formal and direct imitation of the classical details of old Rome. Many notable buildings by the greatest architects of the time—Vignola, Michelangelo, Palladio, and Sammichele—were studiously correct and simple in detail, unlike the free and inventive work of the earlier period. The desire for simple and grand effect led to a new method of treatment, the use of one colossal order embracing two or three stories—the Palladian order, as it is called (PLATE XXIV, p. 222). Palladio was not the first to introduce this treatment, but it was made familiar by a book which he wrote upon the subject, which was widely read in England, and greatly influenced our architecture in this direction. No Italian architect has left his impress so strongly upon English architecture as Palladio. Possibly his influence was, in part, due to the fact that he taught, better than any one else, the method of obtaining good effect cheaply and simply,—that he could make a design "grand without great dimensions and rich without much expense," by the somewhat unworthy use of plaster or stucco with which he coated his buildings. As a reaction from this severer style the Renaissance in Italy ended by combining the picturesque with classic architecture itself; the blend of these produced the Baroque style. "Other architectures, by other means, have conveyed strength in repose. These styles may be grander and of an interest more satisfying and profound. But the

PLATE XXIV — *Palazzo Prefettizio, Vicenza — by Palladio*

laughter of strength is expressed in one style only—the Italian baroque architecture of the seventeenth century." [7]

The baroque still holds its place as the architecture of pleasure—of the garden and the theatre. In Italy, in the hands of such architects as Maderna (p. 219) and Borromini, it produced much tasteless and unsatisfactory work: but under the greater architects it achieved great things. Few buildings are so pleasing in exterior effect, and in the sense of fitness and harmony with the surroundings, as the great baroque church of Santa Maria della Salute, on the grand canal in Venice (PLATE XXV, p. 224), designed by Longhena in 1632 and built to commemorate the cessation of the plague. One does not criticise the details of a design such as this: one says of it, as Vasari said in praise of a building, that it was "not built, but born."

FRANCE.—While the Italian architects were busily reviving the old national architecture, in their own country, the Gothic style in France was vigorous and full of vitality; and for a long time the Renaissance movement had no effect upon it. But at the end of the fifteenth century, when the wars of the French kings brought them into contact with the Renaissance palaces of Italy, the monarchs became fired with ambition to imitate these splendid residences, and brought back in their train several Italian architects, whom they employed to reproduce, to some extent, the great palaces of their own country. In France, however, the foreign artists could not have things their own way.

[7] Geoffrey Scott, "The Architecture of Humanism."

PLATE XXV — *Santa Maria della Salute, Venice*

They introduced many classical details, but the national Gothic traditions were very strong, and for a long time only the minor details could be introduced, while the general plan and composition of the designs continued to be unaffected.

There ensued, then, a long period of transition, when classical details were grafted upon Gothic designs, in the way we find them at the château of Blois. Here the portion which was built for Louis XII, about 1500, shows a curious blending of the styles: the general impression is of a Gothic building, but the new influences are distinctly seen in the mouldings and in the strongly emphasised horizontal lines. It was not until the reign of Francis I, when the new architecture became fashionable, that the classical forms began to assert themselves and to dominate the design. The beautiful Transitional work of this period, the "Francois Premier," as it is called, is full of charm, differing from the Renaissance of Italy in three characteristic features, as the result of the influence of Gothic tradition in France. These special features are (1) a picturesqueness of composition and of outline; (2) the steep-pitched roof, with the natural development of dormers and high chimneys; and (3) lack of symmetry and of formality of plan.

The best examples of the Francois Premier style are the palaces built by the king himself—the north wing of the château of Blois (1525) with its famous external staircase, the great palace of Fontainebleau, and the château of Chambord. At Chambord (1526) we find greater formality of plan than was usual during the earlier period, and an elaborate roof—almost overweighing the design—with a multitude of dormers and tall chimneys, crowned in the centre with a fantastic lantern.

FIGURE 84 — *Dormer, Château of Chambord*

At Chenonceaux, Azay-le-Rideau, and elsewhere dotted throughout the district of Touraine, the delightful châteaux of the nobility bear witness to the memorable times when Francis held his court on the banks of the Loire. In most of these, as also in the château of Mesnières, near Dieppe, we find the same

FIGURE 85 — *Château of Mesnières*

characteristics—steep roofs and elaborate dormers, angle tourelles, and emphatic horizontal string-courses and cornices. The greatest undertaking of the reign, however, was the rebuilding of the Louvre in Paris, which was put in hand about 1545, shortly before the death of Francis. Serlio, an Italian, had been consulted about the designs, but the work was entrusted to a French architect, Pierre Lescot, under whom half the palace— comprising two sides of a vast courtyard—was erected. The work progressed throughout various reigns down to the time of Louis XIV (1660), and was not actually finished until the middle of the nineteenth century, when Napoleon III added the north and south façades. Thus completed, the Louvre is the most extensive of all European palaces, and supplies an excellent record of the progress of French Renaissance. The design has two main stories, with Corinthian order of pilasters below and composite above; over these is a low attic story. Some of the sculptured work, by Jean Goujon, is especially good. The well-known imposing Corinthian colonnade of the east front, almost 600 feet in length (1688), was the work of the court physician Perrault.

Another building of the early period was the Hôtel de Ville in Paris, begun about 1550 from the designs of an Italian, but since destroyed by fire. In the great palace of the Tuileries, designed for Catherine de Medici by Philibert Delorme (1564), several features were introduced for the first time in French architecture; two of these—the bands of rustication carved at intervals across the pilasters and the walls, and the broken pediments of the attic story crowned with statuary—became specially characteristic of later French Renaissance. The introduction of the broken pediments, in imitation, perhaps, of Michelangelo's work in the Medici chapel at Florence, was probably due to Catherine's suggestion. Be that as it may, the idea found favour with the French, and the feature has remained popular with them to the present day.

Towards the end of the sixteenth century the architecture had lost much of the early charm of the Transitional period, and many of the buildings of Henry IV (1589–1610) are coarse in detail and inferior in design: the least interesting portions of the Louvre and of the Tuileries date from this period. Of a little later date are two great French palaces which should be noted—the Luxembourg (1615), with a façade rusticated like the garden front of the Pitti Palace in Florence, and the palace at Versailles, built at enormous cost for Louis XIV by J. H. Mansard (1645–1708), a vast, uninteresting pile, with singularly monotonous façades, and—if we except the chapel—with hardly a redeeming feature in its design. By the same architect, but a more successful design, is the Hôtel des Invalides in Paris, with a great central dome like that of S. Paul's in London. The lofty external cupola is constructed of wood covered with lead; the true dome, of stone, is built on a smaller scale inside. In all these designs of the later Renaissance it will be noticed that there is greater formality, symmetry, often stateliness of design, but a lack of the picturesque charm of the earlier period. One special feature of the Gothic style, however, was always retained in the French buildings—the steep-pitched roofs; and in the seventeenth and eighteenth centuries the massive "Mansard" roof formed a very prominent feature in the design.

GREAT BRITAIN.—Gothic architecture, we have seen, had run its course uninterruptedly in England for many centuries, little disturbed by foreign influences. True, the "Tudor" Gothic of the sixteenth century was a somewhat degenerate form, but it was producing many fine buildings and the domestic mansions of the style— such as we find at Haddon Hall, in Derbyshire (about 1540)—were well suited to the hospitable requirements of the time. It was natural, therefore, that there should have intervened, as in France, a long and interesting period of transition before the newly imported classical details could displace the older Gothic forms.

This Transitional period commenced practically with the reign of Elizabeth (1558), when the court began to give much attention to classical studies, and to introduce numerous foreign artists and craftsmen. At this time, and especially during the early part of the century, there were enormous numbers of foreigners in England—French, Dutch, Italians, and others; in fact, the presence of so many aliens led to a good deal of unpleasantness and even to riots. The native workmen complained then—as they have complained ever since—that the foreigners brought over numbers of ready-made articles, which they sold in this country, and thus lessened the amount of work to be done by the native craftsmen. In this way, in the first instance, foreign ideas and minor classical details began to find their way into the country. Perhaps the first important step in this direction, however, was the employment of the Italian artist Torrigiano, in 1512, to design the tomb of Henry VII in Westminster Abbey, a design which he carried out in the style of his native country. Similarly an Italian would design, in his own Renaissance manner, a chimney-piece here, a monument there, so that the classical forms became, as in France, familiar first through the medium of such accessories. The screen and stalls (1535) in King's College Chapel, Cambridge, are a fine early example of the new style. As classical culture came more into vogue, books upon Renaissance art and architecture were translated from Italian into English, and were freely read. Under these influences the Gothic features tended to disappear, and a clothing of classical orders began to adorn the wall surfaces and

PLATE XXVI — *The Long Gallery, Haddon Hall*

entrance doorways. Soon these became incorporated in the design, while the forms and details underwent a gradual change, as the builders came more and more under the sway of the new movement.

The noble mansion of Elizabeth's time, the familiar "Tudor-chimnied pile of mellow brickwork" belongs to this Transitional period. In examining one of these buildings it is interesting to note how the classical details gradually crept in, while the general Gothic disposition was at first unaffected. At Haddon Hall (1540) the Tudor element predominates, passing, in the later additions and alterations, into the earliest Elizabethan. Here we see the characteristically English feature, the great square bay window, divided into smaller lights by a number of mullions and transomes (PLATE XXVI, p. 231). The influence of the Perpendicular Gothic is seen, too, in Hardwick Hall, where the design is almost overpowered by the enormous windows, so that the rhyme,

> Hardwick Hall,
> More glass than wall,

seems to be literally true. The pierced parapet, which crowns the building, is a feature of frequent occurrence: in places we find it pierced into patterns; sometimes the piercing takes the form of a sentence or motto. At Hardwick the design shows the initials, E.S., of Elizabeth, Countess of Shrewsbury, who built the mansion. Wollaton Hall, Notts (1590), has an early example, in the parapet, of the fantastic "strap" ornament, a feature quite peculiar to English Renaissance. The angle tower of Wollaton in the illustration shows also the free use of the three orders, and the method in vogue of clothing the wall surfaces with classical details.

FIGURE 86 — *Tower, Wollaton Hall*

Inside the Elizabethan mansions the prominent features were the broad, massive staircase of oak or, less frequently, of stone, and the great hall, panelled or hung with tapestry, with open timber roof, bay windows, and minstrels' gallery. In larger mansions a great gallery was often found on the first floor, extending, in some cases, the whole length of the building, as at Montacute House, near Yeovil, where the gallery is 20 feet wide and no less than 170 feet in length.

Few mansions of the period are more interesting than Burghley House, in Lincolnshire, built for the celebrated Lord Burghley. On the building there are several dates, ranging from 1577 to 1587, so that it probably took about ten years, between these dates, to build. Letters which have been found referring to the building, from Lord Burghley to the builders and workmen, throw some light upon the manner in which building operations were carried on in those days. The workmen wrote direct to the employer for instructions, and all the details of the design were referred, not to the architect, but to the employer himself. The latter would settle many questions without outside assistance, but for some of the more important features he would obtain sketches or suggestions from different architects in London, so that the ideas of several architects might thus be embodied in the same building. In Burghley House the greater part of the design is the work of John Thorpe, an architect who was at the time head of his profession.

In many of the designs a good deal of the personal element was introduced: the builders were not hampered by restrictions, and, if a designer had what he considered a happy idea, he was free to embody it in his design, so that we occasionally find quite childish freaks perpetrated. In an interesting collection of sketches and

PLATE XXVII — *The Mote House, Downton*

(Early Eighteenth Century)

notes by John Thorpe, in the Soane Museum, London, there are some careful studies of the orders, and some plans and drawings of a house which Thorpe designed for himself. The plan of the building is in the form of the designer's initials, J.T., the two portions of the building being connected by a corridor. Beneath the plan he had written:

> These two letters, J and T,
> Joined together as you see,
> Is meant for a dwelling house for me.

Although in some of the more classical designs the plans were symmetrical, in other cases the arrangement was quite fanciful. Montacute House, with its vast gallery, already referred to, showed a plan not uncommon in those days, in the shape of the letter E—perhaps a courtier's graceful compliment to Queen Elizabeth (Plate XXVII, opposite). But the courtiers took care, whatever the plan, that comfort was not sacrificed to appearance, believing, with Bacon, that houses were made "to live in, not to look on," and the interior arrangements were excellently designed to cope with the lavish hospitality which prevailed in the "spacious days" of Elizabeth. Very suggestive of the open house are the legends often found carved amongst the ornament; thus, over the front entrance at Montacute: "And yours, my friends"; while round the garden porch run the words: "Through this wide opening gate, none come too early, none return too late."

Among other famous Elizabethan mansions may be mentioned Longleat in Wiltshire, Penshurst and Knole House in Kent—the latter remodelled in the reign of

PLATE XXVII — *Garden Front, Montacute House*

(Late Sixteenth Century)

James I—and Kingston House, Bradford-on-Avon, a replica of which fitly represented English architecture in the Rue des Nations at the Paris Exhibition of 1900.

During the reign of James I (1603–1625),—the "Jacobean" period,—classical forms were used more freely than ever; or perhaps we should say, forms of classical origin, for the details were so distorted and caricatured as to be barely recognisable. Audley End (1603–1616), erected by the Earl of Suffolk, in Essex, one of the most notable mansions of the period, is said to have been designed from a model brought from Italy at a cost of £500; but the style was so modified in transmission that, in 1669, we find Prince Cosmo's secretary—an Italian—criticising the design, and failing to recognise in it the architecture of his native land. "The architecture of the palace," he says, "is not regular, but inclined to Gothic, mixed with a little of the Doric and Ionic." If, then, a contemporary Italian failed to recognise the style of the period, though it had been introduced from his own country, it is small wonder that we find difficulty in tracing and accounting for all the forms and features. Certainly this Elizabethan and Jacobean work is one of the most curious and puzzling transitional styles known in history. Buildings of the same date show an extraordinary diversity in both the amount and the character of the classical features introduced. In some cases the designs are mediæval buildings with the Gothic details left out, and a good deal of uncertainty as to what classical forms should be put in their place. Evelyn, when visiting Audley End, noted it in his diary as a "mixed fabric betwixt ancient and modern, and, without comparison, one of the stateliest in the kingdom"; and Samuel Pepys was puzzled by the architecture, but admired "the stateliness of the ceilings and the form of the whole, and drank a most admirable drink, a health to the King."

It was but natural that this confusion should end in a reaction, and a return to the more correct and dignified use of the classical orders. The man under whose influence the disorder gave way, and who may be styled our first great Renaissance architect, was Inigo Jones.

Inigo Jones (1572–1652) had studied in Italy, especially at Vicenza, the birthplace of Palladio, where he came under the influence of that great master's work. Returning to England, he endeavoured to introduce the monumental style of Palladio, and in the Duke of Devonshire's villa at Chiswick, one of his first works, he reproduced, on a smaller scale, Palladio's Villa Capra at Vicenza. His great opportunity appeared to have arrived when he received the commission to design an immense palace at Whitehall for Charles I. The designs for this great building, and the noble composition of the Banqueting Hall—the only portion erected—are sufficient to place Inigo Jones amongst the foremost masters of the Renaissance. The treatment of this façade, with its two rusticated stories ornamented with pilasters and engaged columns, is suggestive of Palladio, who, as we noticed, frequently superimposed his orders, instead of grouping two stories under one order in the so-called Palladian style.

More fortunate in his opportunities than Jones was his great successor, Sir Christopher Wren (1632–1723), the great central figure in English Renaissance history, who left his impress so unmistakably upon the new London which sprang up after the great fire. Wren was thirty-four years of age, and had just made a name for himself as an architect, when the great fire of London in 1666 cleared the field for him. One of his earliest works completed after the fire was Temple Bar, erected in 1670, and removed two centuries later (in 1878), in which we had an excellent example of his style, and of his judicious use of ornament. In connection with his ecclesiastical work it must be remembered that Wren was called upon to build large churches hurriedly, and at a very small cost. His church designs were hampered by various considerations, and invariably by lack of funds, but he succeeded, almost without exception, in obtaining good effect in a simple and inexpensive manner.

Before the old Gothic cathedral of S. Paul was destroyed by fire, Wren, who had been instructed to survey it, had given an adverse report, in which he stated that the columns were giving way under the weight of the heavy roof. He made various recommendations, but the debate upon his report dragged out, in the usual way, for many months, and nothing was really done until the question was finally settled by the great fire and the total destruction of the building. In a striking passage in Evelyn's diary, dated August 27th, 1666—six days before the fire broke out—he states that he, with Wren and several experts, surveyed the structure that day, and concluded that a new building was necessary; "and we had a mind," he says, "to build it with a noble cupola, a form not as yet known in England, but of wonderful grace." Some years passed, however, before the committee could settle whether the ruins should be restored on their old lines, or whether an entirely new design should be erected; and it was not until 1675 that the new cathedral was put in hand.

As with S. Peter's at Rome, Wren's original plan was a Greek cross, with four equal arms; but the authorities would not agree to this departure from the ecclesiastical form, and it was accordingly extended unto a Latin cross. In the exterior design we see two stories of the Corinthian order but the upper story is a sham, for it is merely a screen with nothing behind it. A deceit such as this detracts from the architectural merit of the design, though it adds a dignity which would otherwise be lacking to the composition. The west front, and the dome, resting upon a lofty drum, surrounded by a fine peristyle, are the most successful features, leading most critics to endorse Fergusson's encomium. "The exterior of S. Paul's," he says, "surpasses in beauty of design all the other examples of the same class which have yet been carried out; and, whether seen from a distance or near, it is, externally at least, one of the grandest and most beautiful churches in Europe." S. Paul's has the advantage over S. Peter's in that it was completed within the space of thirty-five years, under the superintendence of one architect. S. Peter's, on the other hand, suffered from various interruptions, and occupied a century and a half in building, while twenty popes and a dozen architects had a hand in its construction.

The illustration shows the method by which, in S. Paul's, the dome is built up. The inner cupola is carried up in brickwork almost in the form of a hemisphere, with an opening 20 feet wide at the top. The dome, as we see it from the outside, is constructed on a much more imposing scale, in woodwork covered with lead; a brick cone, built up between these two, carries the heavy stone lantern. Thus the "dome," which forms so conspicuous a feature is, in reality, merely a sham; the true masonry domes—the structural portions—are the inner cupola, and the central cone, which is invisible.

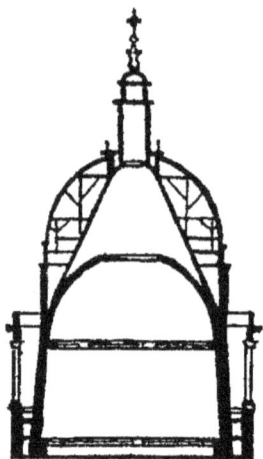

FIGURE 87 — *Section through Dome, S. Paul's*

As construction, and, indeed, as architecture, this feature in S. Paul's cannot compare with the domes at Florence and at Rome; there is not the same honesty of treatment. Wren had never seen either of these Italian domes, but he was doubtless familiar with the method of their construction. Had he been given a free hand, he would probably have built upon these earlier Italian principles; but he was influenced by considerations of expense, and his method was certainly the cheaper of the two.

The interior of S. Paul's is hardly so impressive as the exterior, but this is the fault of the style. It does not disappoint in quite the way S. Peter's does, for it is on a smaller scale, and one does not expect such great impressions from it. The internal effect of the dome is marred by the excessive relative lengths of the nave and of the choir. At first, on entering, one is hardly conscious of the dome; after approaching it, the great length of the choir detracts from its grandeur.

In Wren's numerous London churches he showed great skill in the use of simple materials, and in making the most of the limited funds at his disposal. In many designs the most successful features were the steeples, which he may claim to have been the first to introduce to English Renaissance architecture. A notable example is the beautiful and finely proportioned steeple of Bow Church, Cheapside. But the steeple belongs more truly to Gothic architecture, where it forms an appropriate crowning feature of the whole design. The emphatic horizontal lines which mark all classical compositions render the Renaissance steeple, with its diminishing stories piled one upon the other, somewhat of an anomaly. In S. Stephen's, Walbrook, we have a

FIGURE 88 — *Steeple of S. Mary-le-Bow, Cheapside*

good example of Wren's method of treating the interior of his churches.

The Sheldonian Theatre at Oxford, the southern portions of Greenwich Hospital, Trinity College library, Cambridge, and the garden front of Hampton Court Palace, are among Sir Christopher Wren's most important secular works. His genius is more evident in such buildings as these than in his London churches. It would be too much to expect of any man that he should be successful in the designs of half a hundred churches, all built at the same time, and from limited funds. It would seem that Wren monopolised the work of the latter half of the seventeenth century, for during this very active period there was hardly a building of any importance which did not come from his hands. With the eighteenth century new names come into prominence, notably Hawksmoor, Wren's pupil, who succeeded to his practice, Vanbrugh, and Gibbs. Hawksmoor gave us the London churches of S. George, Bloomsbury, and S. Mary Woolnoth; Gibbs, the interesting designs of S. Mary-le-Strand and S. Martin-in-the-Fields. The greatest work of Sir John Vanbrugh was the mansion of Blenheim—the nation's gift to the Duke of Marlborough—designed in the ponderous symmetrical style which the architect affected, and which is seen again in Castle Howard, Yorkshire. In the less important domestic buildings a pleasing type of simple square-built house was developed during the first part of the eighteenth century (PLATE XXVII, p. 235). This Queen Anne or Georgian house has

PLATE XXVIII — *Interior, Church of S. Stephen, Walbrook (Wren)*

PLATE XXIX — *Church of S. Martin, Ludgate (Wren)*

always formed a good model for later generations of architects: it greatly influenced also the early "Colonial" architecture of the United States.

Important architecture in England during the greater part of the eighteenth century was, to a large extent, a matter of names. The architects were greatly under the influence of Palladio, whose drawings had been published and were greatly in vogue. Under his lead there was a tendency, even in domestic buildings, to sacrifice everything to symmetry and stateliness. Bacon's dictum was reversed, for the houses were now "built to be looked on, not lived in." With all this, however, there was comparatively little noteworthy architecture produced. The work of the century, taken as a whole, shows little originality or high artistic merit; nothing more can be said of it than that it was a respectable sort of architecture, hovering between dignity and dulness.

Among the later architects of the century, Sir William Chambers designed the most important building of the time, Somerset House (1776), which he remodelled from designs of Inigo Jones, and treated in the refined style which marked everything that left his hands. A greater work—through its wide influence over successive generations of students—was his book, a "Treatise on Civil Architecture." Of this period also are the Mansion House, London, by George Dance, senior; the Bank of England, by Sir John Soane; Kedleston Hall in Derbyshire, by Robert Adam—one of the four brothers who gave their name to the elegant "Adam" style of interior decoration which they introduced—and old Newgate Prison, by the younger Dance, a vigorous and appropriate design, now replaced by the Central Criminal Court.

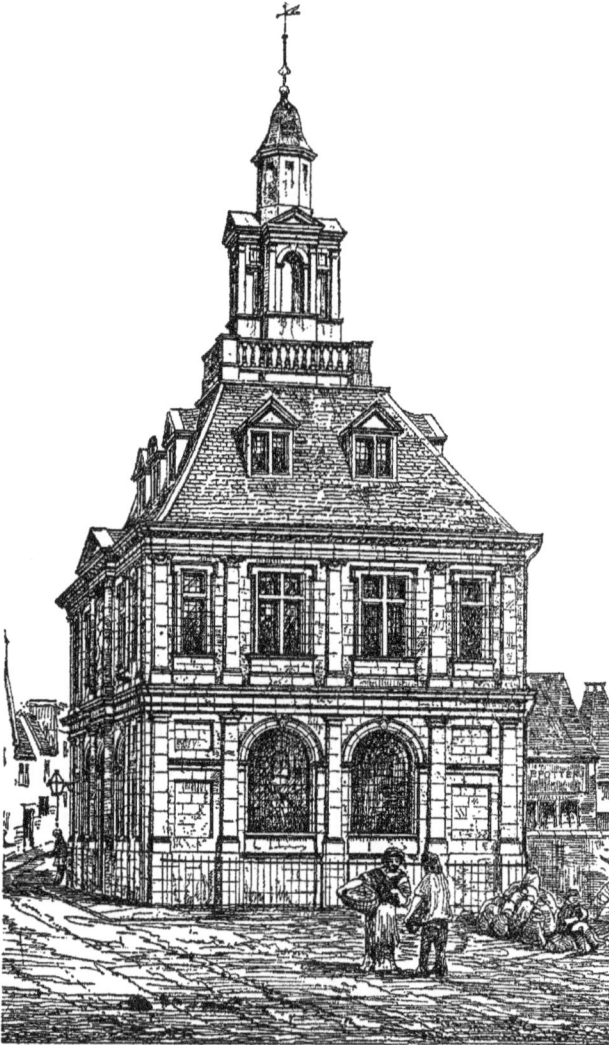

Drawn by W. Bassett Saila.

FIGURE 89 — *The Custom House, King's Lynn (1683)* —
A good example of English Renaissance

CHAPTER IX

MODERN ARCHITECTURE

In comparison with the enormous strides which were made during the nineteenth century in all branches of science, the progress of architecture in that period was slow and lacking in interest. Throughout the continent of Europe comparatively few notable buildings were produced. In France, as we have noted, the Louvre was completed, and the Opera House was built in Paris (1863–1875). Austria produced, among several fine public halls and theatres, the great Opera House, and the House of Parliament (1843) in Vienna, and the Dresden Theatre, all designed more or less on classical lines. German architecture in the early part of the century received an impetus under Schinkel (d. 1841), who designed the Museum at Berlin, with its great portico of Ionic columns, and the Court Theatre, also in Berlin, in which the Greek forms are admirably adapted to the requirements. Other well-known buildings are the Propylæa at Munich, and the Walhalla at Ratisbon—a copy of the Parthenon, by von Klenze (1784–1864). "In general," writes Hamlin, "the Greek revival in Germany presents the aspect of a strong striving after beauty, on the part of a limited number of artists of great talent, misled by the idea that the forms of a dead civilisation could be galvanised into new life in the service of modern needs. The result was disappointing, in spite of the excellent planning, admirable construction, and carefully studied detail of these buildings, and the movement here, as elsewhere, was foredoomed to failure."

In England the past century was one of successive revivals. Each of the three great styles—Greek, Gothic and Renaissance—had its day; but it is only within comparatively recent years that any definite progress has been made towards the formation of a distinct national style of architecture. In the early part of the century the interest aroused by the publications of Stuart and Revett and others upon the monuments of Greece, and the importation of the Parthenon sculptures by Lord Elgin, led to a craze for Greek details. Doric and Ionic orders were used in connection with every design, without any regard to propriety, provided only they were of strictly correct detail and proportions. Every house had its classical portico, every church was a slavish copy from a Greek model. In the church of S. Pancras, London, the architect reproduced the Caryatid Porch of the Erechtheum at Athens, and copied his steeple from the Temple of the Winds. The revived Greek style found its highest expression in S. George's Hall, Liverpool, by Elines and Cockerell; and so closely were the classical details adhered to in this building that, in Fergusson's words, "the architect failed in his endeavours if you are able to detect in S. George's Hall any feature which would lead you to suppose the building might not belong to the age of Augustus."

Meanwhile, a small band of enthusiasts had been preparing the way for the revival of the neglected and almost forgotten Gothic architecture. The publication of Britton's great work on "The Cathedral Antiquities of England" caused many people to reflect that, after all, Gothic was the great national style, and, as such, was more suited to the English requirements than the Greek temple forms could possibly be. Rickman's book upon the Gothic styles followed, and the movement, once in progress, soon gained strength. It did not lack great leaders—writers as well as designers: Pugin, Street, and, weightiest of all, Ruskin, threw their influence into the scale, and the Gothic revival became an established fact. It produced many notable buildings; chief among them the Houses of Parliament at Westminster, begun by Sir Charles Barry in 1839, in the Perpendicular style, and the New Law Courts in London, by Street.

But while the Gothic movement was at its height, the Greek school had by no means become extinct. The two styles were being worked out simultaneously in a way that was quite unprecedented. At Liverpool the classical style was culminating in S. George's Hall, begun in almost the same year (1840) that saw the inception of the Gothic Houses of Parliament in London; moreover, the architect of the Gothic building was at the same time busy with such classical designs as the Treasury buildings and the Reform Club. Small wonder, then, that there resulted a great "Battle of the Styles," which was waged fiercely between the opposing parties. It was especially bitter over the great competition for the Government Offices in 1857, the result of which, to quote the late J. M. Brydon's words, "was quite typical of the ding-dong of party warfare. Won by a classical design, the decision was annulled in favour of a Gothic building, to be reversed again in its turn, and finally carried out in classic by a Gothic architect against his will."

Good work in the free Gothic style was done towards the end of last century by J. L. Pearson in Truro Cathedral, and several London churches; and by Alfred Waterhouse, who adapted the style successfully to public buildings such as the Town Hall and the Law Courts, Manchester.

During the last part of the century, however, and since, there has been witnessed in England, and, indeed, through Europe, a return to the Renaissance principles, seen in a large number of designs in which the classical forms are treated with freedom and, later, with skilful adaptation to new requirements and new methods of construction. In Great Britain it began with what is called the Queen Anne revival, followed by "Free Classic," in which the architect was able to express his individuality without being too much hampered by tradition. In the hands of capable artists such as Norman Shaw and Ernest George, there was a gradual renaissance of architecture as a *personal* art. As a result this country produced many mansions and domestic buildings unsurpassed for their happy blending of dignity with charm. Among public buildings, Norman Shaw's New Scotland Yard (A.D. 1891) on the Thames Embankment, is a bold and daring example.

The closing years of the nineteenth century fore-shadowed the vast influence which the extensive use of iron and steel was to exercise in the future upon architectural works and upon the forms of design. In the course of the present century great progress has been made in respect of building methods and organisation, so that it is now possible to build more rapidly, and to complete a structure in far shorter time, than in the past. Commercial buildings are now becoming nothing more than gigantic frameworks of iron and steel, covered with a clothing of masonry. "For thousands of years," as a recent writer puts it, "every large building in the world was constructed with enormous walls of masonry to hold up the inner framework of floors and partitions. It was a substantial and worthy method of construction, and there seemed no need of changing it. But one day a daring builder, with an idea, astonished the world by reversing this order of construction, and building an inner framework strong enough to hold up the outside walls of masonry. The invention was instantly successful, so that to-day the construction of a tall building is 'not architecture, but engineering with a stone veneer.' "

CHAPTER X

ARCHITECTURE TO-DAY

In the present day all avenues are open to the student of architecture. Knowledge is no more a fountain sealed. Even to the slender purse the greatly increased facilities for travel, and the improved means of communication of all kinds, make it possible to visit fields of study which, in the days of Wren and Inigo Jones, were inaccessible to all but the favoured few. The classical buildings of imperial Rome, the mediæval churches and cathedrals of Europe, the palaces of the Renaissance in Italy, and the châteaux on the banks of the Loire in France,—with all these the student may make himself acquainted, not only by travel but by means of drawings, photographs, and literature. And to the great army of travellers, not necessarily students, these scenes are becoming increasingly familiar.

The result of all this is a certain cosmopolitanism in architecture throughout the civilised world. In all the principal cities one finds mammoth hotels, all modelled upon sumptuous lines, to cater for the same international guests; while theatres, public buildings, and business premises tend to approximate to the one type. Some architects, indeed, have practices which extend into other countries than their own, so that we find French- or Paris-trained artists designing buildings in England, architects of Great Britain carrying out their designs for all parts of Europe and in India, and Americans at work on both sides of the Atlantic. This, again, leads to a fusion of styles in different and distant countries.

The recognition of the importance of town-planning, and the wide and general interest taken in the scheming and the growth of garden cities, the popularity of exhibitions dealing with the home and with all that pertains to the home, the revived joy in the garden and its rehabilitation as an appropriate frame and setting to a building, all indicate a growing regard to things architectural.

The general use, in modern days, of steel and iron has an enormous influence upon the disposition and the design of almost every important building. In an earlier chapter we noticed that, in the great baths and basilicas of imperial Rome, the marble and the bricks formed but a coating to the solid concrete structure and had little constructional value. So, with our modern building methods, there is a tendency, and an increasing tendency, towards concealment, and, one might say, deception; and it is probable that, with the rapidly expanding uses of steel and concrete, the present century will witness a revolution in the art of building. Almost every important building, be it county hall, theatre, or public office, is designed with its network of steel framing, which forms the real skeleton of the structure upon which it depends for its stability. The advantages of such methods of construction are obvious, as, for example, in a hall or theatre, where it becomes possible to dispense with all visible means of support for the balconies, and thus provide an uninterrupted view of the stage from every part.

The special method of construction which has become established during recent years, and which is in process of extraordinary development, is that known as armoured or reinforced concrete. This consists of fine cement concrete strengthened by light steel bars of various forms embedded in it. Reinforced or ferro-concrete has been successfully used for a long period in important engineering works, and in this utilitarian twentieth century is destined to come into very general use in the construction of the more important buildings of this and every great country, and to influence greatly the design of the architect as well as the engineer. In London it may be regarded as a sign of the times that the great stone classical façade which Sir Robert Smirke, the designer of the Mint and the British Museum, built for the General Post Office in S. Martin's-le-Grand, has been pulled down, while in the new Post Office we have a great public building constructed throughout in ferro-concrete, and faced with masonry. The later structure is doubtless the more enduring type of building, for, as the ruins of ancient Rome show, good concrete will stand the stress of centuries without any apparent loss of strength.

The lessons of the earthquakes at San Francisco and Messina have not been lost upon architects and engineers, and it is likely that great additional stability will be given to buildings in cities similarly situated, by means of the constructive methods of armoured concrete.

France continues to make her refining influence felt in all artistic matters throughout the world, and exercises specially a controlling interest in the educational training of the architects of the United States, many of whom, if they have not actually studied at the *École des Beaux-Arts,* have at any rate gone through a course of training at one of their national technical colleges, where the curriculum is founded upon that of the great Paris school. Modern French buildings display the grace and charm which clever artisans, acting under well-trained, if not inspired architects, can give to fine conceptions. The rigid system of study which the ambitious French architect pursues, and the serious consideration and thought which he is encouraged to devote to the solution of big problems during his course, fit him to think in a large and generous way, and to approach the working out of great schemes with confidence and skill.

Moreover, in the sympathetic interest of the Government in the advancement of the Arts, he finds great encouragement. As a result, we have in the modern hôtel-de-ville a type of building of great interest and architectural merit, in which dignity and use are combined. The hôtel-de-ville corresponds to our municipal building or town-hall, but in France the administrative requirements are not so complicated as in England, nor so utilitarian. In England the chief problem of the architect is to accommodate in the most practical and comfortable manner the numerous officials with their staffs, assigning to each department its due proportion of space. The French conditions are less exacting, so that in the hôtel-de-ville a much larger proportion of the space can be devoted to the entrance vestibule and the grand staircase, while the reception apartments are designed on a spacious and imposing scale. Wall-paintings and sculpture, in which architects, painters, and sculptors collaborate, are distinctive features; and as the building is used for civil marriages and for numerous civil functions and receptions, greater attention is given to considerations of effect.

At Sens, Tours and elsewhere, the modern hôtels-de-ville are good examples of the work that the best architects have produced, and are still producing, under encouraging conditions. In these, and in all the best examples, the architecture of France still preserves that appreciation for scale and proportion which has always been its characteristic quality.

A formal classicism pervades the public buildings of Berlin, and the recently completed cathedral there, with its conventional classical forms, presents no features of special interest beyond a certain boldness of plan. Towards the end of last century some of the German and Austrian architects, wearied with the resuscitation of classical forms which, they felt, left them no scope for individuality, became suddenly attracted to the new style of architecture known as l'Art Nouveau. This allowed them to give free play to their fancy, and it was seized upon and travestied by architects of Dusseldorf,

Cologne, etc., with enthusiasm. But recently there has been a return to saner methods, and—before the war—to the study of the later French styles. Some notable buildings have resulted, embodying designs of great interest and promise, as, for example, the Hotel Adlon in Berlin, the Kursaal at Weisbaden, the Law Courts at Munich, and the Festhall at Frankfort, a building in which the architect, von Thiersch, "has met the new traditions of his time, ferro-concrete and the like, and has succeeded in combining with them a scholarly tradition and considerable imagination."

The showrooms of Schneider and Hanan in Frankfort, and the Wertheim premises in Berlin, with their arcaded front on the lower story and perpendicular treatment of the windows above, are exponents of the modern movement. The Berlin Town Hall has a fine tower with some refined and interesting Renaissance detail.

AMERICA. In comparison with older countries all architecture of the United States may be regarded as "modern." At the time of their settlement the American colonies naturally received their ideas of architecture from the Mother-Country, where Gibbs, Hawksmoor, Sir W. Chambers and other followers of Wren were at work. Gibbs also had published a book of his designs, which found its way into the new colonies, and greatly influenced church architecture there. The buildings first erected were chiefly churches and places of worship, and a few mansions. As would be expected, the church designs followed closely upon the lines of their English models, e.g., Christ Church, Philadelphia (1727) and S. Paul's, New York (1766); but as bricks and stone were not at first readily available, nor their use generally understood, the material chiefly used was wood, and the designs and details imported from England were modified to meet this method of construction. The builders thus developed great skill in the adaptation and use of wood in conjunction with brickwork, with the result that a distinct style was evolved, to which the term "Colonial" has been applied. In the domestic buildings the designs based upon the Queen Anne and Georgian styles were similarly treated. Many of the best examples still remain, e.g., Longfellow House in Cambridge (1757) and Sherburne House, Portsmouth (1714); they are all well-proportioned buildings, which their comparative age invests with special interest. Having won her independence, the United States felt an increased need for Government buildings, and, under the influence of the classical revival in England and France, some notable work in this style was projected, including the Capitol and the White House in Washington, the Mint in Philadelphia, and the old Custom House in New York. But the "Battle of the Styles" made its influence felt in the States also, and little progress was made in the evolution of a national style until the latter half of the nineteenth century. Since that time, however, the progress has been extraordinary.

Two architects made their influence felt in the middle of that century, after they had returned from study and experience in Paris—H. H. Richardson and R. Morris Hunt: and to them chiefly was due the vogue for the Paris school which has had such marked effect upon American architecture. Richardson, after his Paris training, had made a careful study of the Romanesque forms of the South of France, and drew especially upon the Romanesque of Auvergne.

The extensive field for building provided by the large number of rapidly developing towns affords the American architect excellent opportunities for the exercise of his art on a grand scale. The demand in the United States for important public buildings by rich communities, the wealth of the commercial magnates, and the natural development of great territories, call for the most ambitious work of their best architects. The destruction of San Francisco by earthquake and subsequent fire, in 1906, testified to the good qualities of the steel-frame building, by proving in a practical manner its better resistance to earth-shocks than edifices more entirely constructed of brick and stone. The rebuilding of this important city took place with remarkable rapidity, and it is to be noted that the style most in favour with the banks and public buildings is classical renaissance. In the United States the architect is not hampered by restrictions such as exist in our large cities, and the characteristic outcome of the utilitarian requirements of the day is the "sky-scraper"—"a steel bridge standing on end, with passenger cars running up and down within it"—which has become a familiar feature in almost every great American city. These gigantic structures were at first regarded merely as engineering problems, without due consideration of their architectural possibilities, but the enterprising

American architects with sound prevision quickly realised that even the sky-scraper had possibilities. The problem was an attractive one, and the successful way in which it has been solved may be appreciated by comparison of the earlier structures with the more recent great Woolworth Building in New York, 765 feet in height, with 60 storeys and 26 lifts (PLATE XXX, opposite); or with the selected designs in the international competition for the Chicago Tribune Building. In every other direction also there has been steady and persistent development of architecture in the United States during the present century. "Anyone who has visited America during recent years," says Professor Reilly, "would not hesitate to place her architecture first among all her great achievements." There are two reasons for this—the method of work of their architects, and the attitude of the public to whom that work appeals. In America, he points out, there is a far greater demand from the public for architecture as a visible and noble expression of modern civilisation: and there are good schools of architectural training in all the universities. The characteristics of the best American architecture are simplicity and refinement, always desirable qualities, but especially in a country which suffers from a lack of competent craftsmen. In whatever direction we look—theatres, hospitals, university, school, and library buildings, hotels and mansions—American Architecture is now in a state of unparalleled development.

Nor do Canada and the other great dominions lag behind. In each country the conditions of life are

PLATE XXX — *Woolworth Building, New York*

being expressed in noble and enduring terms in their Architecture. In the design of the Canadian Bank of Commerce in Montreal is exhibited the Canadian sense of largeness. This building shows an elevation of six enormous Corinthian columns of granite, each eight feet in diameter, and standing sixty feet high.

GREAT BRITAIN.—In Great Britain there are signs of greater interest being taken by the public in things architectural. It is more and more realised that architecture, properly understood, not only concerns the man in the street: it comes home to all householders and households. And in the long run a nation generally gets the architecture it deserves.

Considerable thought is being given by our architects to planning, and the scientific side of architecture has progressed equally with the æsthetic. Many noteworthy buildings have arisen in the course of the present century. The Roman Catholic Cathedral in Westminster is a good example of modern brickwork with limited use of stone in a Byzantine style, and of the employment of concrete for forming the domed roofs. The London County Council Hall is a notable addition to the Thames-side: and in such buildings as the Metropolitan Water Board Offices, the Institute of Chemistry, Adelaide House, adjoining London Bridge, and many bank premises in London, and public offices at Cardiff, Bristol and other great centres we find architectural development, expressed by originality of treatment and fitness for their special requirements.

Bush House, Aldwych, is a good example of

commercial architecture, designed by American architects with due regard to the neighbouring buildings. Some of the great business premises which have been, and are being, erected in London and elsewhere—designs with great columns carrying a

PLATE XXXI — *The Strand and Aldwych, London, showing a modern improvement area*

bold entablature—may be said to have established a new scale in street architecture. Modern Church architecture finds its freest and highest expression in the new Cathedral Church of Liverpool, a building which, when completed, will take its place worthily among the historic Cathedrals of England. "The whole design"—to quote the words of His Majesty The King at the recent ceremony of consecration—"brings out the grandeur of the architect's conception and the skill with which he has solved the problem of adapting the buildings to the noble objects it has to serve."

British architecture to-day is strong and sane, and healthy. Architects who are, happily, still with us, are producing excellent work which does not need to fear comparison with any other country. When posterity sets itself to praise famous men, there are names among these which will not be forgotten. In London, as throughout all the country, there is evidence of an architectural re-birth.

"In the past twenty-five years," [8] says an American writer, "London, for example, has been transformed into one of the most architecturally impressive cities of Europe. And not in the way of aping in more or less perfunctory a fashion the splendours of imperial Rome: but in a spirit of artistic individual enterprise, and with that courage even to make mistakes, provided the end be liberty, that befits the Metropolis of self-governing Dominions."

---

[8] C. H. Caffin.

A BRIEF LIST OF
BOOKS RECOMMENDED
TO STUDENTS

General Reference

BELCHER, J.—Essentials in Architecture

CAFFIN, C. H.—How to Study Architecture

CHOISY, A.—Histoire de l'Architecture

FERGUSSON, J.—History of Architecture of all Countries

FLETCHER, SIR B.—A History of Architecture on the Comparative Method

GODFREY, W. H.—A History of Architecture in London

GOTCH, J. A.—The Growth of the English House

HAMLIN, A. D. F.—History of Architecture

PERROT and CHIPIEZ.—History of Ancient Art. Vols. on Ancient Chaldæa, Egypt, Phrygia, Primitive Greece, Phœnicia, etc.

PHILLIPPS, L. MARCH.—The Works of Man

PHILLIPPS, L. MARCH.—Form and Colour

SCOTT, GEOFFREY.—Architecture of Humanism

SIMPSON, F. M.—A History of Architectural Development

STATHAM, H. H.—A Short Critical History of Architecture

STURGIS, R.—A Dictionary of Architecture and Building

STURGIS and FROTHINGHAM.—History of Architecture

VIOLLET-LE-DUC.—Dictionnaire de l'Architecture Française

Egyptian and Assyrian

BELL, E.—Egyptian Architecture

CHOISY, A.—L'Art de bâtir chez les Egyptiens

MASPERO, G.—The Dawn of Civilisation

MASPERO, G.—Art in Egypt

PETRIE, W. F.—The Arts and Crafts of Ancient Egypt

PETRIE, W. F.—Ten Years' Digging in Egypt

PLACE, V.—Nineve et L'Assyrie

PRISSE D'AVENNES, E.—L'Art Egyptien

RAGOZIN.—Chaldea

Cretan and Greek

ANDERSON, W. J., and SPIERS, R. P.—The Architecture of Greece and Rome

EVANS, SIR A. J.—The Palace of Minos

D'Espouy, H. — Fragments de l'Architecture Antique

Gardner, E. A.—Ancient Athens

Gardner, P.—Grammar of Greek Art

Hawes.—Crete: The Forerunner of Greece

Lethaby, W. R.—Greek Buildings

Marquand, A.—Greek Architecture

Penrose, F. C.—Principles of Athenian Architecture

Stobart.—The Glory that was Greece

Stuart and Revett.—Antiquities of Athens

Etruscan and Roman

Anderson, W. J., and Spiers, R. P.—The Architecture of Greece and Rome

Dennis, G.—The Cities and Cemeteries of Etruria

Lanciani, R.—Ancient Rome in the Light of Recent Discoveries

Middleton, J. H.—The Remains of Ancient Rome

Rates.—Restaurations des Monuments Antiques, publiées par l'Académie de la France à Rome

Stobart.—The Grandeur that was Rome

Strong, Mrs. A.—Roman Sculpture

Taylor and Cresy.—The Architectural Antiquities of Rome

Early Christian

CHOISY, A.—L'Art de Bâtir chez les Byzantins

CLAUSSE, G.—Les Monuments du Christianisme au Moyen Age

FROTHINGHAM, A. L.—Monuments of Christian Rome

HUBSCH, H.—Monuments de l'Architecture Chretienne

LETHABY, W. R., and SWAINSON, H.—Church of Sancta Sophia, Constantinople

MARUCCHI, O.—Basiliques et Eglises de Rome

MONOGRAPHS OF THE BYZANTINE RESEARCH FUND:—Monastery at Phocis; Church of the Nativity at Bethlehem; St. Eirene, Constantinople

SALZENBURG, W.—Alt-Christliche Baudenkmäler von Constantinople

TEXIER, W., and PULLAN, R. P.—Byzantine Architecture

Saracenic

BOSWORTH-SMITH, R.—Mohammed and Mohammedanism

JONES, OWEN.—Plans, etc., of the Alhambra

PRISSE D'AVENNES, E.—L'Art Arabe

SPIERS, R. P.—Architecture East and West

Romanesque

CATTANEO, R.—Architecture in Italy from the VI th to the XI th Centuries

CUMMINGS, C. A.—History of Art in Italy

HAUPT, A. VON.—Die Baukunst der Germanen

JACKSON, SIR T. G.—Byzantine and Romanesque Architecture

McGIBBON, D.—The Architecture of Provence

PORTER, A. K.—Mediæval Architecture

VENTURI, A.—Storia dell'Arte Italiana, Vols. II and III

Gothic

BOND, F.—Gothic Architecture in England

BOND, F.—Cathedrals of England and Wales

BOND, F.—An Introduction to English Church Architecture

GARNER and STRATTON.—Domestic Architecture during the Tudor Period

JACKSON, SIR T. G.—Gothic Architecture in France, England and Italy

LETHABY, W. R.—Mediæval Art

PARKER, J. H.—Glossary of Terms used in Gothic Architecture

PRIOR, E. S.—Gothic Art in England

ROSE, E. W.—Cathedrals and Cloisters of Midland France

RUSKIN.—Stones of Venice

STREET, G. E.—Account of Gothic Architecture in Spain

STREET, G. E.—Brick and Marble in the Middle Ages in Italy

Renaissance

ANDERSON, W. J.—Architecture of the Renaissance in Italy

BELCHER, J. and MACARTNEY, M. E.—Later Renaissance Architecture in England

BIRCH, G. H.—London Churches of the XVII th and XVIII th Centuries

BLOMFIELD, SIR R.—History of French Architecture, 1494–1661 and 1661–1774

BLOMFIELD, SIR R.—History of Renaissance Architecture in England

BRIGGS, M. S.—Baroque Architecture

FLETCHER, SIR B.—Andrea Palladio: His Life and Works

GOTCH, J. A.—Early Renaissance in England

GOTCH, J. A.—The English Home from Charles I to George IV

GOTCH and BROWNE.—Architecture of the Renaissance in England

RICHARDSON, A. E., and GILL, C. L.—London Houses, 1660–1820

SIMPSON, F. M.—History of Architectural Development. Vol. III

VENTURI, A.—L'Architettura del Quattrocento

WARD, W. H.—Architecture of the Renaissance in France

WREN, SIR CHRISTOPHER.—Memorial Volume

Later Renaissance

ADAM, R. AND J.—Works in Architecture

CHANDLER, J. E.—Colonial Architecture of Maryland, Pennsylvania and Virginia

EBERLEIN, H. D.—Architecture of Colonial America

EMBURY, A.—American Churches

RICHARDSON, A. E.—Monumental Classic Architecture in Great Britain and Ireland during the XVIII th and XIX th Centuries

INDEX

Abbaye-aux-Dames, 137.

Abbaye-aux-Hommes, 134.

Adam Brothers, 247.

Alberti, 207.

Alhambra, 117.

American Progress, 260.

Amiens Cathedral, 158, 173.

Arch of Constantine, 76-77.

Arches, early examples of, 11, 25, 57, 59.

Arnolfo del Cambio, 190, 202.

Assyrian Column, 25.

Assyrian Remains, 24.

Audley End, Essex, 238.

Ball-flower Ornament, 167.

Baroque Architecture, 221.

Basilica of Constantine, 84.

Basilicas, 82-83, 90.

Baths of Caracalla, 81.

Baths of Diocletian, 81.

Beauvais Cathedral, 161.

Beni-Hasan, Tombs at, 9, 11.

Blenheim Palace, 244.

Blois, Chateau of, 225.

Bradford-on-Avon, 141, 238.

Bramante, 213, 217.

Brunelleschi, 190, 202-205.

Burghley House, 234.

Byzantine Dome, 101, 103.

Cancellaria Palace, 216, 217.

Canterbury Cathedral, 170, 171.

Capital, Abbey Church, 131.

Capital from Persepolis, 27.

Capital, S. Germain des Prés, 156-157.

Capital with dosseret, 99.

Castle Rising Church, 145.

Certosa at Pavia, 192, 213.

Chapter-houses, 179.

Chartres Cathedral, 157.

Cheops, Pyramid of, 5.

Chevet, 132.

Church of the Apostles, Cologne, 138.

Circus Maximus, 75.

Cleopatra's needle, 14.

Cloaca Maxima, 59.

Cloister, S. Paul Outside-the-Walls, 91, 92.

Cologne Cathedral, 197-198.

Colonial Architecture, 260.

Colosseum, 74.

Colour Decoration in
  Temples, 23, 46.

Composite Capital, 66.

Concrete in Roman buildings, 64.

Corinithian Capital, 65-66.

Corinthian Order, 55, 66.

Cretan Excavations, 28.

Custom House, 243.

Cyclopean masonry, 33, 59.

Development of Basilica, 95.

Doges' Palace, 194-195.

Dome of St. Paul's
  Cathedral, 241-242.

Dome of St. Peter's, 220

Doric order, 38, 46.

Dosseret, 99.

Duomo at Florence, 202.

Durham Cathedral, 143-144, 182.

Earl's Barton, Saxon work at, 141.

Early Christian builders, 90.

Egyptian Columns, 22-23.

Egyptian Inscriptions, 16.

Elgin marbles, 45, 48.

Elizabethan mansions, 232.

English cathedral plan, 168, 174.

Ephesus, Temple at, 54.

Erechtheum, 52, 53.

Etruscan tombs, 60.

Evelyn's diary, 238.

Fan-tracery, 179.

Fire of London, 240.

Florence Cathedral, 190.

Flying Buttress, 152, 153.

Foscari Palace, 196, 197.

Franciscan monks as builders,
  189.

Giotto's Campanile, 193.

Glass, Painted, 155, 177.

Golden House of Nero, 71.

Gothic, Meaning of, 130.

Gothic Revival, 251.

Gothic Ribbed Vaulting, 149.

Greek Temple Plan, 37, 39.

Griffin Fresco at Knossos, 33.

Haddon Hall, 229, 231.

Hagia Sophia, 101-103.

Hardwick Hall, 232.

Henry VII, Tomb of, 230.

Honey-comb Corbelling, 113.

Houses of Parliament, 251.

Hypostyle Hall at Karnak, 17, 20.

Inigo Jones, 239.

Ionic order, 49, 50.

John Thorpe, 234.

Karnak, temples at, 14, 16.

King's chamber, 6.

King's College Chapel, 180.

Knossos, Palace of, 31, 32.

Leaning tower at Pisa, 125-126.

Lighting of Greek temples, 37.

Lincoln Cathedral, 175-179.

Lion-gate, Mycenæ, 33-34.

Liverpool Cathedral, 266.

Lotus-bud Capitals, 13, 22.

Louvre, 227.

Lucca Cathedral, 128.

Luxor, Temples at, 14.

Lycian Tombs, 49-50.

Maison Carrée, Nîmes, 73.

Mansard roof, 229.

Mausoleum at Halicarnassus, 57.

Michelangelo, 218.

Mihrab, or Prayer Niche, 112.

Milan Cathedral, 192.

Minoan Civilisation, 30.

Mohammed, 110.

Monreale Cathedral. 128.

Montacute House, 236.

Mosaics, Use of, 96-97, 104.

Mosque of Kait Bey, 113-114.

Mosque of Sultan Hassan, 113, 116.

Mosques, 112.

Mouldings, Gothic, 184.

Narthex, 83, 91.

Norman Work, Examples of, 148.

Norman work, Features of, 147.

Notre Dame du Port, 131-133.

Opera House, Paris, 249.

Opus Alexandrinum, 97.

Orders of Greek Architecture, 38.

Orders of Roman Architecture, 66.

Palladio, 221, 247.

Pantheon, 78-80.

Parish churches in England, 181, 184.

Parthenon, 39, 41, 43, 46.

Pavia, Certosa at, 192, 213.

Pazzi Chapel, Florence, 206.

Pepys, Samuel, 239.

Persepolis, Ruins at, 26.

Petrie's discoveries in Egypt, 21, 87.

Pompeian decoration, 86.

Pompeian houses, 85.

Pyramids, 4-5.

Ramessium, 219.

Ravenna, Churches at, 98.

Ribbed vaulting, 149.

Roman Entablature, 76-77.

Romanesque, Contrasted with Gothic, 152.

Roman temple Plan, 67.

Rusticated Masonry, 210, 229.

S. Clemente, Rome, 98.

S. Francesco at Assisi, 189.

S. Francesco at Rimini, 209.

S. George's Hall, Liverpool, 250.

S. Maria della Salute, 223, 224.

S. Maria delle Grazie, 212-213.

S. Maria Novella, 207-208.

S. Mark's, Venice, 106-108.

S. Martin-in-the-Fields, 244.

S. Mary-le-Bow, 243.

S. Mary's Chapel, 145.

S. Pancras, London, 250.

S. Paul-Outside-the-Walls, 91-92.

S. Paul's Cathedral, 237-239.

S. Peter's, 217-220.

S. Sophia, 102-104.

S. Stephen, Walbrook, 237-239.

S. Zeno, Verona, 123.

Sainte Chapelle, Paris, 151.

Salisbury Cathedral, 173, 174.

Saxon Remains, 141.

Sculpture, Greek, 46.

Shepherd Kings of Egypt, 12.

Sky-scrapers, 261.

Spinelli Palace, 215.

Steel Construction, 255.

Stokesay Castle, 183-184.

Stone Tomb, Lycia, 49.

Strand and Aldwych, 265.

Strasbourg Cathedral, 197-198.

Strozzi Palace, 210

Temple Bar, 240.

Temple of Ramses, Karnak, 16.

Temple of Wingless Victory, Athens, 53.

Theatre of Marcellus, 69-70.

Theatres, Greek, 56.

Thebes, 13, 19.

Theseum, 39, 47.

Tiryns, Walls at, 33.

Tracery, Development of, 155, 177, 179.

Transepts, Origin of, 96.

Treasury of Atreus, 34.

Triumphal Arches, 76.

Tudor Gothic, 229.

Unfoliated Early English Capital, 184.

Ur of the Chaldees, 24.

Vandalism in the Middle Ages, 72.

Vicenza: Palazzo Prefettizio, 222.

Vocal Memnon, 16.

Westminster Abbey, 176.

Whitehall Palace, 239.

Wingless Victory, Temple of, 53.

Wollaton Hall, 232-233.

Woolworth Building, 262.

Worms Cathedral, 139.

Wren, Sir C., 240.

Xerxes, Hall of, 26.

Ypre: Old Cloth Hall, Frontispiece